T0060280

THE MIND OF MAHĀMUDRĀ

The Mind of Mahāmudrā

Advice from the Kagyü Masters

Translated and introduced by

Peter Alan Roberts

Series editor
Thupten Jinpa

WISDOM PUBLICATIONS • BOSTON

Wisdom Publications
199 Elm Street
Somerville, MA 02144 USA
www.wisdompubs.org

Library of Congress Cataloging-in-Publication Data
The mind of Mahamudra : advice from the Kagyu masters / Translated by Peter
Alan Roberts ; Edited by Thupten Jinpa.
    pages cm. — (Tibetan classics)
  Includes bibliographical references and index.
  ISBN 978-1-61429-195-4 (pbk.: alk. paper) — ISBN 1-61429-195-0 (pbk. : alk.
paper) — ISBN 978-1-61429-212-8
  1. Spiritual life—Bka'-brgyud-pa (Sect) 2. Mahamudra (Tantric rite) 3. Meditation—Buddhism. I. Roberts, Peter Alan, 1952– translator. II. Thupten Jinpa, editor
of compilation.
  BQ7679.6.M56 2014
  294.3'4435—dc23

                              2014013965

ISBN 978-1-61429-195-4   ebook ISBN 978-1-61429-212-8

18 17 16 15 14
5 4 3 2 1

Cover and interior design by Gopa & Ted2, Inc. Set in Diacritical Garamond Pro
10.7/12.7. Cover image is "Painting of Karmapa Rangjung Dorje," courtesy of the
Rubin Museum Collection.

Wisdom Publications' books are printed on acid-free paper and meet the guidelines
for permanence and durability of the Production Guidelines for Book Longevity of
the Council on Library Resources.

This book was produced with environmental mindfulness. We have elected to print
this title on 30% PCW recycled paper. As a result, we have saved the following
resources: 10 trees, 5 million BTUs of energy, 850 lbs. of greenhouse gases, 4,609
gallons of water, and 309 lbs. of solid waste. For more information, please visit our
website, www.wisdompubs.org.

Printed in the United States of America.

MIX
Paper from
responsible sources
FSC
www.fsc.org   FSC® C011935

Please visit www.fscus.org.

Publisher's Acknowledgment

THE PUBLISHER gratefully acknowledges the generous contribution of the Hershey Family Foundation toward the publication of this book.

Contents

General Editor's Preface

IT's A true joy to see the publication of *The Mind of Mahāmudrā* among the select paperback volumes of the *Tibetan Classics* series. The six translations featured here offer clear explanations of the famed Buddhist meditation practice known as *mahāmudrā*, "the great seal." At its heart, mahāmudrā involves the use of a direct method of seeing the nature of the mind—as it is, without and beyond subject-object duality and conceptualization. It's a simple yet profound practice that has been the focus of many great masters of both India and Tibet.

The texts featured in this volume have been drawn from the larger *Mahāmudrā and Related Instructions: Core Teachings of the Kagyü School*, which appeared as part of *The Library of Tibetan Classics*. The translator Peter Alan Roberts has produced a new introduction for this special volume, as well as provided short explanations at the beginning of each of the six texts. Along with the explanatory notes and glossary, these ancillary materials will greatly help the general reader engage with these important Tibetan texts in a deeper and more meaningful way. I offer my great thanks to Peter for his masterful translations of the texts and for the care and dedication with which he has striven to make this volume such a gem.

I would like to express my deep gratitude to Khenchen Thrangu Rinpoche for his guidance and counsel in the compilation of this volume. My heartfelt thanks also go out to Eric Colombel and the Tsadra Foundation for the generous support that enabled the translation of *Mahāmudrā and Related*

Instructions, the source for this paperback anthology. I must also thank the Hershey Family Foundation, the Ing Foundation, and Pierre and Pamela Omidyar for their generous support of the Institute of Tibetan Classics. Last but not least, I would like to thank Tim McNeill and his team at Wisdom Publications for their dedication to these classics series, and David Kittelstrom, our long-time editor at Wisdom on the classics series, whose incisive editing always helps bring a level of clarity to our volumes that would otherwise not be there.

May this volume be a source of joy and spiritual wisdom to many seekers on the path.

Thupten Jinpa
Montreal, 2014

Translator's Introduction

THE SIX TEXTS compiled in this volume address the subject of *mahāmudrā*, the central meditation practice of the Kagyü school of Tibetan Buddhism.[1] They were written in classical Tibetan between the twelfth and the seventeenth centuries.

Mahāmudrā is essentially a simple, direct method for seeing the nature of the mind. This method of meditation appeared in northern India in the last centuries of the first millennium and was introduced into Tibet in the eleventh and twelfth centuries by both Indians and Tibetans, and these various transmissions became absorbed into the Kagyü tradition. Khenchen Thrangu Rinpoche (b. 1933), the foremost scholar in the Karma Kagyü tradition today, selected the eleven texts that comprised the larger volume this book is distilled from.[2]

In the Kagyü tradition, the higher tantric practices are two-fold—the *stage of generation* and the *stage of completion*.[3] The generation stage entails the visualization of oneself as an enlightened deity within a divine palace encircled by an entourage; and the practice consists primarily of visualizations, mantras, prayers, and offerings. The practitioner's habituation to "pure perception" of the deity and the environs eliminates ordinary habits of perception and reveals the intrinsic purity of all mental and physical phenomena.[4]

The Kagyü school divides the completion stage into two kinds of practice: the path of methods and the path of liberation. The *path of methods* consists primarily of the six Dharmas of Nāropa,[5] and the *path of liberation* is primarily the practice of mahāmudrā, the topic of the present volume.

Mahāmudrā, or *chakchen* (*phyag chen*) in Tibetan, literally means "the great seal." Masters of this tradition have explained it to mean that everything is sealed with buddhahood, the intrinsic true nature, which is already perfect. Therefore there is nothing to be added to or removed from the mind. There is no liberation to be attained other than what is already present. A common saying is that the reason why mahāmudrā is not attained is not because it is too difficult but because it is too easy, not because it is too far but because it is too close, and not because it is hidden but because it is too evident.

Therefore the mahāmudrā tradition employs the phrase "ordinary mind" to express that enlightenment is nothing other than the mind that we already have. As Tselé Natsok Rangdröl states in his text within this volume, the error that meditators make is "thinking that simply maintaining the 'ordinary mind'—your own mind—is not enough. Instead you seek elsewhere for some longed-for, imagined, marvelous meditation."

The actual meditation entails looking inward, directly at one's own mind, without conceptualization, categorization, or conclusions. This true nature of the mind is there for anyone to see, and anyone who looks in this way will inevitably see it, at least for an instant, before conceptualization sets in. The practice of the meditation is essentially familiarization with this direct seeing of the mind.

Nevertheless, a series of graded meditations are taught in conjunction with this practice, including basic śamatha meditations, for stabilizing concentration, and successive stages of *vipaśyanā* meditation, insight practices that lead a practitioner gradually to actual mahāmudrā.

Thrangu Rinpoche has emphasized on many occasions that the Sixteenth Karmapa, Rikpé Dorjé (1924–81), told him that mahāmudrā was the most beneficial practice for Westerners because it eschews complex and culturally foreign practices. Rinpoche has also stated that elaborate practices such as the six

Dharmas of Nāropa and dark retreats do not achieve any higher goal than mahāmudrā but are taught for the benefit of those who cannot believe that the ultimate attainment can be attained by such a simple method. Nevertheless, he adds that pursuing an array of practices can aid practitioners in their progress.

Mahāmudrā in India

The term *mahāmudrā* had earlier uses in Buddhist literature,[6] but it first appears as synonymous with buddhahood in such higher tantras as the *Buddhakapāla Tantra*, which is said to have been revealed by Saraha (ninth–tenth century).[7] Saraha's songs or *dohas* are considered to be the source of the mahāmudrā lineage, and therefore Saraha is said to be the first human teacher of mahāmudrā.

The *doha* is a literary medium most closely associated with Indian mahāmudrā teachings and was used by successive generations of siddhas in India. However, the meaning of the word *doha* was lost in Tibetan translation. A *doha* is in fact a particular form of rhyming couplet. Famous examples of dohas are the Hindi poetry of Kabir (1440–1518), in which each doha could be an independent separate work. Indian poetry employed various kinds of verse and meter based on patterns of long and short syllables, unlike Tibetan, which counts only the number of syllables per line. As there is no Tibetan equivalent for the word *doha*, it has often simply been transcribed rather than translated. However, the general word for a spiritual song in Tibetan is *gur* (*mgur*), and the dohas along with a related type of verse called *caryāpādas* written in the earliest form of Bengali are generally referred to in Tibetan as *gur*. This has led to an inaccurate back translation of all instances of *gur* in Tibetan, including native Tibetan songs, as *doha*, glossed as "a song expressing realization."

Saraha's dohas were written in an eastern form of Apabhraṃśa and appear to actually be a collection of couplets by various authors. The *do* in *doha* means "two." Their distinctive rhyming sound pattern is lost in their Tibetan translation. For example:

Brāhmaṇ to nā jāne to bhed
Ebhāve pāḍ ā hoḥ e catur ved

(For brahmans do not know the truth
but simply recite the four Vedas.)

Saraha is said to have transmitted his mahāmudrā lineage to the siddha Nāgārjuna, the tantric master whom the Tibetan tradition conflates with the well-known Mādhyamika of that name. Śavaripa, described as a pupil of both Saraha and Nāgārjuna, is said to have been a hunter from the tribal peoples in what is now Orissa. In one description of how Śavaripa first appeared to his disciple Maitripa, he is wearing a peacock-feather skirt and attended by two tribal women picking lice from his hair.

We enter surer historical footing with Maitripa (986–1063),[8] who became the principal master of mahāmudrā in India. Maitripa studied with Nāropa for twenty years and is said to have started teaching in his fifties. His hermitage appears to have been in Mithilā, an area around the present border between Bihar and Nepal.

Marpa Chökyi Lodro came from Tibet and received mahāmudrā instructions from both Maitripa and Nāropa (956–1040).[9] Nāropa was one of the most famous Buddhist masters in India in the first half of the eleventh century. A surprising first-hand description of Nāropa in the final years of his life describe him as corpulent, his hair dyed red with henna, chewing betel and being carried on a palanquin.[10] What we know about Nāropa's teacher Tilopa (928–1009) comes primarily through the legends of his disciple's life. One of Tilopa's dohas is popularly known as the "Ganges Mahāmudrā" because it was recited to Nāropa on the banks of the Ganges.[11]

The Introduction of Mahāmudrā into Tibet

Atiśa received mahāmudrā instruction from Maitripa, which must have been before 1040, the year of both Nāropa's death and Atiśa's departure for Tibet via Nepal. He arrived in Tibet in 1042, where he stayed until his death twelve years later at age seventy-two. He taught mahāmudrā to his pupil Dromtön (1004–63), but Dromtön decided against making mahāmudrā a part of the Kadam tradition, fearing it would have a negative influence on conduct.[12]

The mahāmudrā lineage of Marpa Chökyi Lodrö (eleventh century),[13] even though he was a pupil of Maitripa and the ostensible founder of the Kagyü tradition, is classed as the *subsidiary translation tradition* (*zur 'gyur*), because initially other mahāmudrā transmissions, many of which originated with Vajrapāṇi (b. 1017),[14] were of greater importance.

Dampa Kor Nirūpa (1062–1102) was a Tibetan who held yet another mahāmudrā lineage. After becoming the object of the practice of *purapraveśa*, or "entering another's body," Dampa Kor, as he was originally called, became known as Kor Nirūpa. A practitioner and traveler to Nepal from an early age, Dampa Kor is said to have died there when he was only nineteen. In the same house at the time was seventy-three-year-old Nirūpa, a pupil of Maitripa's disciple Karopa. Nirūpa performed the practice of *purapraveśa* and entered Dampa Kor's body and revived it. After Nirūpa's old body was cremated, he went to Tibet in the young Tibetan body but wearing Indian clothing and with the conjoined name of Kor Nirūpa. He then changed to wearing Tibetan clothing and taught mahāmudrā there for twenty-one years, dying at age forty, this time in the more conventional manner.

Following these earliest transmissions of mahāmudrā there came what are called the *middle transmissions*, in which Vajrapāṇi, another disciple of Maitripa, plays a crucial role. Vajrapāṇi moved to the Kathmandu Valley in 1066, and went to Tibet with his Kashmiri pupil Dharmaśrī and gave many teachings in the Tsang region. Eleven texts in the Tibetan canon are attributed to him. The lineage of his teachings is called the *upper* or *western* mahāmudrā tradition to differentiate it from two other mahāmudrā traditions, the *lower* and *later* mahāmudrā.

The *lower* or *eastern* mahāmudrā began with Vajrapāṇi's pupil, a Nepalese brahman generally known as Asu.[15] Asu is said to have been passing through Tibet on pilgrimage to China when he married a Tibetan woman and settled down in the Phenyul area. Asu had many pupils and established a family line of mahāmudrā through two of his four sons.

Asu taught mahāmudrā to Milarepa's pupil Rechungpa (1084–1161), who also studied with Rāmapāla, one of Maitripa's four principal pupils, and with Tipupa, one of Maitripa's seven "middle-ranking" pupils.[16] Rechungpa introduced various teachings into Tibet, even transmitting them to his own teacher, Milarepa. Rechungpa's transmission is central to the Drukpa Kagyü school, which originated with Lingrepa, who was at one time a practitioner within Rechungpa's nonmonastic lineage.

The *later* tradition of mahāmudrā comes from Nakpo Sherdé, a pupil of Vajrapāṇi in Nepal during the master's last years. He focused in particular on the dohas of Saraha.

Mahāmudrā instructions were also introduced into Tibet in the twelfth century. Vairocanarakṣita, a paṇḍita originally from South India, studied in northern India under a number of masters, the most famous being Abhayākaragupta (d. 1125), the greatest Indian Buddhist master of his time. Vairocanarakṣita's principal teacher for mahāmudrā was the great scholar and yogin Surapāla at Nālandā, who taught him the *Twenty-Six Teachings of Non-attention*.[17] Vairocanarakṣita became a master of mahāmudrā as well as other tantras and visited Tibet a number of times, eventually dying there. He translated many mahāmudrā dohas and teachings, including those of Maitripa. His pupils in Tibet are said to have included Lama Shang (1122–93), one of this volume's authors.[18]

The Kagyü Schools

The Kagyü is one of the major traditions of Tibetan Buddhism. Soon after its establishment in the eleventh and twelfth centuries, it branched into a number of independent Kagyü schools. Buddhism had been introduced into Tibet in the seventh and eighth centuries during Tibet's dynastic period, and that early tradition is called *Nyingma*, or "old." By the eleventh century, the Tibetan kingdom had fragmented, and Tibetans went on their own individual initiative to India in search of teachings unavailable in Tibet, particularly what were called the *highest yoga tantras*, which had appeared in India in the ninth and tenth centuries. The schools formed in Tibet from that time onward are collectively called *Sarma*, meaning "new."

The Kagyü, which literally just means "lineage of instructions," considers its founder to be Marpa, and Marpa Kagyü is a generic name for all Kagyü lineages. Marpa spent many years visiting India and Nepal, studying under Nāropa and Maitripa in particular. In Tibet Marpa became a wealthy landowner, in contrast to the ascetic lifestyle of his pupil Milarepa (ca. 1040–1123),[19] who became the subject of the most popular biography in Tibet's religious history.[20] A biography of Milarepa and a collection of his songs were composed and compiled in the late fifteenth century by Tsangnyön Heruka[21] (1452–1507). This exceptional writer also composed a popular biography of Marpa.[22] But while they are powerful biographies, neither is reliable in terms of historical veracity. Unlike earlier biographies that portrayed Milarepa as an emanation of a buddha, Tsangnyön presents him as an ordinary being who has to overcome many obstacles in order to achieve enlightenment, and therefore this biography has been the source of inspiration for practitioners from all traditions.

Milarepa spent much of his life in solitary retreat in mountain caves, and most of his principal pupils led the same kind of lifestyle, including his main pupil, Rechungpa (1084–1161).[23] Rechungpa is significant for the history of the Kagyü in that he also visited India and introduced a number of mahāmudrā and other teachings into the lineage.

The first Kagyü monastery was founded by Milarepa's pupil Gampopa Sönam Rinchen (1079–1153), also known as Dakpo Lhajé, and the many schools that derive from him are called the Dakpo Kagyü.[24] He was originally a monk from the Kadam tradition, which focused on the foundational ethical teachings and practical application of the sutras, de-emphasizing the higher tantras. Gampopa's union of two apparently antithetical traditions and his establishment of a monastic community as a foundation for Milarepa's practices created the basis for the widespread and powerful monastic Kagyü traditions. Tsangnyön's fifteenth-century biography of Milarepa casts Gampopa as Milarepa's principal pupil, declaring him to be the "sun-like" disciple and Rechungpa as the secondary "moon-like" disciple.[25]

Gampopa, with his scholastic background, was the first in the Kagyü school to author a significant number of texts. His substantial text on the graduated path entitled the *Ornament of Precious Liberation* continues to be an essential foundation for Kagyü study.[26]

Gampopa's successor as abbot of his monastery was his nephew Gomtsul (1116–69),[27] short for Gompa Tsultrim Nyingpo, whom he had adopted as a ten-year-old boy and declared to be the rebirth of an Indian paṇḍita.[28] Gomtsul became directly involved in resolving religio-political conflicts in Lhasa. He rebuilt the main temple in Lhasa, which had been destroyed, and established law and order in the Lhasa region.

Lama Shang (1122–93) was a pupil of Gomtsul and he continued this secular activity, firmly establishing theocratic rule over the region. He also founded Tsalpa Monastery and the Tsalpa

Kagyü, which no longer exists as an independent school. However, this volume contains two Tsalpa Kagyü texts, one of which is by Lama Shang himself.

Of the more than fifteen Kagyü lineages that have appeared since the eleventh century, those that currently survive as major independent schools are the Karma Kagyü, Drukpa Kagyü, and Drigung Kagyü. The Drukpa Kagyü exists in both Tibetan and Bhutanese forms. Its most famous lama, Pema Karpo, is the author of one of our mahāmudrā texts.

The largest Kagyü tradition is that of the Karma Kagyü, which was founded by Düsum Khyenpa (1110–93), a pupil of Gampopa and Rechungpa. He became the first in a series of recognized reincarnations, the Karmapas,[29] becoming the earliest in the now ubiquitous *tulku* system of incarnate lamas. Among numerous other tulkus to appear within the Karma Kagyü tradition, the Shamarpas and Situ Rinpochés have been the most consequential. Gampopa, Lama Shang, and Düsum Khyenpa all recognized lamas and children as rebirths of great masters, but the Second Karmapa, Karma Pakshi (1204–83), was the first to inherit the monasteries and authority of his predecessor. The Third Karmapa, Rangjung Dorjé, is the author of two our texts in this volume.

As for the smaller, yet still existing Kagyü lineages, the Barom Kagyü continues to have over a dozen monasteries in Golok, a region in the northeast of the Tibetan plateau. The Taklung Kagyü had a major monastery and lineage in both central and eastern Tibet and still continues in a reduced form. In eastern Tibet the Yelpa Kagyü, Yasang Kagyü, and Trophu Kagyü continue to have a few monasteries and tulkus. The Martsang Kagyü has presently no monastery, but its principal tulku and the transmission of its essential teachings continues.[30] The Shuksep Kagyü transformed into a Nyingma tradition, with a famous nunnery. There are also the Surmang Kagyü and Nedo Kagyü, though they function as subschools within the Karma

Kagyü.[31] The Shangpa Kagyü is technically a distinct, separate lineage from the Marpa Kagyü traditions, but while it can be classified as a school in its own right, it is currently primarily preserved as a lineage of practices within the Karma Kagyü.

Acknowledgments

It has been a great privilege to take part in this visionary work of Thupten Jinpa, whose intelligence and motivation is only matched by his patience. Khenchen Thrangu Rinpoche, whom it has been an enlightening delight to translate for during two decades, chose these texts, providing me with a challenge on several levels to live up to Samuel Beckett's dictum "Fail better." Without the beneficence of Eric Colombel's Tsadra Foundation, I would not have been able to even take my first step on this road. I am particularly indebted to the late Gene Smith and all the workers at the Tibetan Buddhist Resource Center (TBRC), who have made the life of a translator many gigahertz easier. Christian Chartier, who has translated *Mahāmudrā and Related Instructions* into French, has been an invaluable aid in revising my English translations. Vienna University's website Resources for Kanjur & Tanjur Studies has enabled the mystery of the source of certain quotations in the first edition to be solved, or to be resolved to truly be mysteries.

Many have helped me to be able to reach the stage where I could attempt this work, in particular the late Akong Rinpoche, who set me on the path of learning Tibetan; the late Tibetan language teacher Tenpa Gyaltsen Negi; and Professor Richard Gombrich, who taught me Sanskrit and Pali at Oxford University. I am thankful for the help in understanding various passages that I have received directly from Alak Zenkar Rinpoche, Khenchen Thrangu Rinpoche, Lamchen Gyalpo Rinpoche, Yongey Mingyur Rinpoche, Karl Brunnhölzl, Sarah Harding, Edward Henning, and Lodro Sangpo. I am also thankful I had the indispensable guide of a previous translation of Tselé Natsok Rangdröl's text by Erik Pema Kunsang. And I have greatly benefited from the works of such scholars as Alexander Berzin, Hubert Decleer, Elizabeth English, David Gray, Christopher Lindtner, Dan Martin, Kurtis Schaeffer, Andrew Skilton, Jikido Takasaki, and Shinichi Tsuda.

In particular, thanks to David Kittelstrom, who with assistance from Lea Groth-Wilson and Laura Cunningham accomplished the unenviable task of editing my work. And a special thanks to my wife Emily Bower for her continuing support, encouragement, and wisdom.

1. The Unrivaled Instructions of Shang Rinpoché

The Preliminaries and Main Practice of the Great Meditation of Mahāmudrā

———∞∞∞———

Shönu Lha

The *Unrivaled Instructions of Shang Rinpoché* is an early teaching on the preliminary practices for mahāmudrā. Preliminaries became central and ubiquitous practices in all schools of Tibetan Buddhism. This presentation is simple compared to later versions; there is no emphasis, for instance, on accumulating manifold repetitions of these practices. The instructions on meditation that follow the preliminaries consist of direct and simple advice on resting the mind in the natural state. It does not explain a graduated path of successive stages of meditation, as is found in later mahāmudrā works.

Not much is known about the author, Shönu Lha (thirteenth century). The work is from the Tsalpa Kagyü lineage founded by Lama Shang (1122–93), the author of the next text in this volume. Its title indicates that it presents instructions passed down from Lama Shang. Shönu Lha was a lama of Pangshong Lhari Monastery and a pupil of Lharipa Namkha Ö, presumably the founder of Lhari Monastery, who was a direct disciple of Lama Shang.

I PAY HOMAGE to the sublime gurus.

> I pay homage to the precious guru.
> The activity of your compassion comes to all beings
> from the state of great bliss, the elaboration-free
>   dharmadhātu,
> and the power of your blessing liberates your pupils.
> I shall write these instructions from the guru exactly as
>   he taught them;
> they are the essence of the Dharma, the highest of all
>   vehicles,
> the inheritance from the great Kagyüpas of the past,
> the practice of the lords, the path that guides pupils.

The principal teaching of the Lord of Dharma, glorious Lha-ripa,[32] is the method for revealing mahāmudrā to be within the grasp of your hand. It is an instruction given to karmically worthy pupils. It is the Dharma of the father of the entire Dakpo Kagyü.[33] It is a sublime secret path; the blessing of the direct introduction that enables you to see nakedly the precious nature of the mind; it reveals to us our inner, innate realization. Here are this tradition's preliminary and main instructions.

My sublime guru established the three levels of vows as the foundation for pupils, ripened them with empowerments, and taught them these instructions. The precious guru gave the following teachings:

We have obtained the precious human body with its freedoms and opportunities. We have no defects in our five senses. While we have this independence, we should accomplish the goal of eternal peace and happiness. In order to accomplish that, we need the Dharma. In order to practice the Dharma, perfect faith is indispensable. In order to develop faith, we must contemplate the defects of samsara and meditate on death and impermanence.

Everyone in the past was born and then died. Everyone who is yet to be born will definitely die. For those of us alive now, it's impossible that only one or two of us will die while the rest of us go on living. We're born and then we die—that's the nature of impermanence. It is said in a sutra:

> It is doubtful that you have ever seen
> or even heard of someone
> on this earth or in a higher world
> who was born but has not died.[34]

The death of every being is terrifying and near. It's impossible that it won't happen. We shouldn't even feel certain that we will still be alive tomorrow morning. Ācārya Śāntideva has said:

> It is not right to comfort myself by thinking
> "I will not die today."
> The time will doubtless come
> when I will cease to exist.[35]

We definitely will die, but we don't know when. The young should not feel certain that they won't die, because in this world there is no definite time for death: a baby dies in one family, a child dies in another. Most people die in adulthood, and only a few don't die until they're old. We have short lives because the lifespan has declined in this degenerate age. Even the few who live a full life only reach sixty. So we can't know whether we will die tomorrow, the day after tomorrow, or next year. Suddenly we are seized by something we have not planned, and, terrified, we die with wildly staring eyes and a hundred goals left unachieved.

From the *Sutra of the Excellent Night*:

> Who knows that they will die the next day?
> Therefore act with dilligence this very day.
> The Lord of Death and his great army
> will be no friend to you.[36]

As soon as we are born from our mothers, we draw closer and closer to our deaths with each passing day. Yesterday has gone and today is going. We cannot stop it, and we only draw closer and closer to dying. Yesterday was impermanent, so now it's today, but today is also impermanent. Since the previous month was impermanent, the current one followed it. Last year was impermanent, and before long it was over. Without our being aware of it, this attacks and destroys us. It is taught in a sutra:

> The flowing water of a rapid river
> moves ever onward, never to return.
> Human lives are the same;
> those who have gone will not return.[37]

And:

> If even the vajra body, adorned with
> the primary and secondary signs, is impermanent,
> then those with bodies that have no essence,
> like plantain trees, are obviously so.[38]

Even the great Śākyamuni, the perfect Buddha, and all the gurus and siddhas of the past died and passed away, so what point is there for us to hope to be permanent? Everyone is heading toward death, and I too will fail to defeat death.

A clever speaker can't prevent passing away. The very wealthy can't avoid it. Even powerful rulers cannot defeat it. Once the conditions for supporting life have ceased, there is nothing anyone can do. Even if you say that you must remain alive for just a little while longer, you will be unable to for even an additional moment. Even though you've amassed great wealth and property, you will leave it all behind and go on alone and empty-handed. Śāntideva has said:

> You may have acquired many possessions,
> amassing them over a long time,
> but you will leave naked and empty-handed,
> just as if a robber has stolen everything.[39]

It's terrifying to be naked, empty-handed, bound tightly by a rotting rope, and forcibly dragged away. Can you endure contemplating your certain death? Even if you have many friends, followers, and servants, you can't send anyone else in your place. You can't postpone death, and there will be no one to go with you; you will have to leave immediately and totally alone, like a hair pulled out of butter. When the time comes, the riches you've accumulated will not help; your friends and relations will not help; whatever mark you've made in this world will not help. You will leave behind every support in this life. Each of us will leave carrying the burden of our ripening karma. This is definitely going to happen. It is taught in *Entering the Conduct of a Bodhisattva*:

> Even though, as I lie upon my bed,
> I am surrounded by friends and family,
> when my life comes to an end,
> I will have to experience that alone.
>
> When the emissaries of Death seize me,
> what can my family do? What can my friends do?[40]

We are definitely going to die and we don't know when. We don't have the time to take it easy, and nothing but the Dharma can help us. Contemplate this and dedicate yourself to the Dharma.

Those who don't understand think, "Death is going to come whether I practice the Dharma or not. Everyone dies, sooner or later, so why should I feel bad about it?" Those who think that way become thoughtlessly involved with this life and don't understand.

How could there possibly be eternal life? There can be happy deaths and unhappy deaths, but those who don't practice the Dharma, whether they die young or old, will not have any happiness in the land of death.

We don't cease to exist at death but are reborn. If you don't practice the Dharma, you will be reborn in the three lower existences. Can you possibly conceive of that suffering? The suffering in the hot and cold hells is inconceivable. It's taught that in the hot hells you suffer for many eons the unendurable torture of being chopped up, cut into pieces, burned in fire, cooked, and beaten. It's taught that in the cold hells, the body freezes, blisters, cracks, splits, and so on.

Pretas suffer from hunger and thirst. It's taught that they don't even see food or drink for months or years. Even when they do see or find some, there is only more suffering, because it is stolen by others or transforms into puss and blood, or weapons rain down on them, and so on. It's taught that because their bad karma is not exhausted, they can't die, and so their suffering is inconceivable.

Animals suffer from being stupid and ignorant. They also suffer from eating each other: there is the suffering of the larger animals eating the smaller ones, the smaller animals eating the larger, the many eating the few, and the few eating the many. The happiest animals are those who are cared for by humans. But they also suffer from being loaded as if they're carts and used against their will. They are sheared, have their noses pierced, are milked, and so on. They are continually used until they are eventually killed. If humans are happy, they make the animals happy; if the humans suffer, they make the animals suffer. They are used as servants until they become old, and then they are taken to the butcher, who returns them with staring, bloody eyes. Then they're eaten. Haven't you seen this suffering?

The three lower existences are nothing but suffering, but it's taught that the three higher existences bring countless sufferings too. The devas have the suffering of falling to a lower existence when their life is over. Their adornments age, their light fades, their deva companions abandon them. They know they are dying. They suffer because they can see with their clairvoyance that their next life is a fall into a bad existence. It's taught that their suffering is unendurable, like fish writhing on hot sand.

The asuras suffer because of fighting or because of being killed, wounded, defeated, and so on. It's taught that they too have countless sufferings.

Humans experience the four great rivers of suffering: birth, aging, sickness, and death. In addition, there's the suffering of taking care of what you have, the suffering of seeking but not finding what you don't have, the suffering of meeting, or being afraid of meeting, aggressive, angry enemies; and the suffering of being separated, or the fear of being separated, from beloved friends. In particular, in this degenerate age, there are such afflictions as Mongolian governors, malevolent leaders, and slavery.

If you don't have good things, that causes unhappiness; if you have good things, that causes suffering; if you have bad things, that causes suffering; having something causes suffering and not having it causes suffering.

Once we are born here in samsara, there is nothing that is beyond suffering, beyond the cycle of suffering, beyond the characteristics of suffering. Maitreyanātha has taught in the *Sublime Continuum*:

> The nature of samsara is suffering.
> Those in samsara have no happiness.
> Its nature is like fire.[41]

If now, during this brief time that we have the precious body of a deva or a human, we don't repel the army of samsara and gain the objective of eternal benefit, who knows where we'll be reborn?

The attainment of this precious human existence is extremely rare. If you hurl peas against a wall as smooth as a mirror, it's unlikely even one will stick to it. Gaining a human existence is even more difficult than that. If you throw peas against a mirror, can even one stick to its surface? No, they all fall. From *Entering the Conduct of a Bodhisattva*:

> [Therefore the Bhagavān] taught that
> obtaining the human existence is as difficult
> as it is for a turtle to stick its neck through the hole
> of a yoke floating on a great ocean.[42]

A yoke floats upon the surface of a great ocean. Once a century, a turtle rises to break the surface with its head. It's extremely unlikely the turtle's head will come up through the yoke. It's even more difficult than that to attain a human existence. Therefore Ācārya Śāntideva taught:

> These freedoms and opportunities are difficult to obtain,
> but human beings have gained this success.
> If they do not accomplish its benefits,
> who knows when they will fully acquire it again?[43]

Thus, it's taught that human existence is difficult to obtain. During the short time we have this fragile human body, it is possible to end our wandering in samsara, so that's what you should do. Perform this great act of kindness to yourself. It's crucial that you don't deceive yourself. Whatever you do, you don't have the leisure to not practice the Dharma.

You must first take vows in order to practice the Dharma, and you have taken them. Now, whether you wander in samsara or attain buddhahood depends on your mind. If you don't know its nature, you wander in samsara; if you do know it, that's buddhahood; so you must know it. What prevents you from knowing it? Bad karma and impurity. To purify bad karma, there is first the hundred-syllable mantra instruction, which is very important and really must be practiced.

Enter a strict retreat in a solitary place, such as in a sealed chamber. Sit upon a comfortable cushion and make a sincere oath, thinking, "Oh! I'm so fortunate that I haven't died before today. Time has passed so quickly without my paying attention. Now I only have the last part of my life left, so during this brief time I must accomplish the goal of everlasting benefit. I shall practice nothing but the Dharma. I shall dedicate what little of my life remains to this purpose. Gurus and the Jewels! Be my witness for this!"

Meditate a little while on death, impermanence, and the faults of samsara, so that you will not remain idle or neutral. Then develop bodhicitta sincerely, thinking, "I will attain buddhahood for the sake of all beings and bring them to the level of perfect buddhahood. For that purpose I will practice the meditation and mantra of Vajrasattva." Then recite three times the bodhicitta prayer that begins "In the Buddha, the Dharma..."[44]

Then clearly meditate that you are the *yidam* deity, with glorious Bhagavān Vajrasattva one forearm's length above your head. Clearly meditate that he is white in color, with one face and two arms. The right hand holds a golden five-pronged vajra to his heart, and the left hand, holding a silver bell, rests upon his hip. He is bejeweled with all precious adornments and is inseparable from the wisdom being (*jñānasattva*). The syllable *hūṃ*, which is on a full-moon disc and lotus in his heart, is the essence of nondual wisdom, the minds of all the buddhas. It is white and shining, the color of mercury. For the sake of all beings, it radiates light in all directions to invoke the essence of nondual wisdom, the minds of all the buddhas of the three times. This essence melts into nectar, which is drawn in from all directions and enters glorious Bhagavān Vajrasattva through the fontanel on the crown of his head, completely filling his body with its whiteness.

The nectar flows out from under the nail of the big toe on his right foot, pouring down to the crown of your head and entering into you. It washes away your bad karma and obscurations, and these come out from your ten toes and your anus in the form of black liquid, like charcoal-stained water. Imagining that, repeat the hundred-syllable mantra about a thousand times.

> *Oṃ vajrasattva, samayam anupālaya, vajrasattva tvenopatiṣṭha, dṛdho me bhava sutoṣyo me bhava, supoṣyo me bhava, anurakto me bhava, sarva siddhim me prayaccha, sarva karmasu ca me cittaṃ śreyaḥ kuru, hūṃ, ha ha ha ha ho, bhagavān, sarvatathāgatavajra ma me muñca, vajrī bhava mahā samaya sattva, āḥ.*[45]

[*Oṃ* Vajrasattva! Protect the commitment! Vajrasattva, you be present! Be steadfast for me! Be pleased with me! Take care of me! Be loving toward me! Bestow all the siddhis upon me! Make my mind good in all my actions! *Hūṃ, ha ha ha ha ho*! Bhagavān, Vajra of all the tathāgatas, do not abandon me! Be a vajra holder! Great commitment being! *Āḥ.*]

When you finish, visualize Vajrasattva merging into you. Then your body and mind become relaxed from within, and you rest unwaveringly in a state of ease. Conclude by sealing it with a dedication.

In general, to practice this meditation and mantra repetition well, the meditator does four practice sessions. At dawn, the third part of the night, think, "Oh! I didn't come to this hermitage so that I could sleep. I didn't come to these mountains so that I could sleep. I did not seal myself into this retreat so that I could sleep. I have slept so much throughout beginningless samsara and I'm still unsatisfied. So sleeping now is not going to give me satisfaction." Get up immediately and start the practice described above. Meditate until it is time for breakfast. At breakfast time, seal your practice with a genuine dedication. Then eat breakfast while practicing the yoga of food.[46] After breakfast, diligently sit on your cushion and practice until lunch. When it's time, again end with a dedication. Apply yourself to practice throughout the afternoon until it is time for the daily *torma* offering. Then practice the complete torma offering, offerings to the Jewels and so on. When the torma has been offered, sit diligently on your mattress. Without lying down, dedicate yourself to practice for the first third of the night: the evening. Seal each evening with dedication and prayer. For the sake of your health, sleep in the correct physical posture for the middle part of the night. At dawn, begin practicing as described.

Always keep to this program of four sessions: the evening, the dawn, the morning, and the afternoon. Spend your day in that way. Spend a month in that way. Spend a year practicing in that way. Spend your entire life dedicated to practicing in that way.

That's how it's taught you should dedicate yourself to practicing the meditation and repetition of the hundred syllables in four sessions.

The supplication to the guru is the principal preliminary practice, which should be done in this way:

In the dawn session, wake early and contemplate death and impermanence. Practice one rosary each of the refuge, bodhicitta, and the hundred syllables, meditating as far as Vajrasattva merging into you, as described above.

In front of you, there should be a mirror mandala, a clay mandala, a wooden mandala, a slate mandala, or whatever kind of mandala you have, with twenty-three heaps of barley arranged upon it. Meditate that you are a deity and your root guru is above the crown of your head. Above his head is his own root guru, and above that guru's head is his root guru, and so on, up to the sixth Buddha, Vajradhara.[47]

Meditate that all space, your entire visual field, is filled with gurus, buddhas, bodhisattvas, ḍākas, ḍākinīs, guardians who are Dharma protectors, and so on, gathered like clouds. Confess your bad actions in their presence by thinking, "I confess and regret all bad actions I have done throughout all my lifetimes, from beginningless samsara until now. I pray that you cleanse and purify me!" Thinking, "You know whether I should be sent upward or downward," put yourself completely into their care.

The mandala serves simply as the basis for the visualization. There is a great ocean upon a ground of gold. In its center is the supreme mountain surrounded by four continents, eight subcontinents, and the seven precious possessions of the cakravartin king, with the open vase of treasure as the eighth. There are the sun and moon, the oceans, the continents, a variety of jewels, a variety of grains, and various mounts, such as horses and elephants. There are wish-fulfilling cows, bathing tanks for washing, unploughed harvests, and different kinds of precious substances such as jewels, gold, silver, lapis lazuli, and *aśmagarbha*,[48] the precious "stone essences." There are countless, unimaginable, specific offerings: varieties of silk adornments, such as parasols, victory banners, flags, and tassels; different kinds of music, such as drums, horns, cymbals, and lutes; myriad sensory pleasures of form, sound, smell, taste, and physical sensations; and possessions that are cherished in the world, such as gold, turquoise, horse harnesses, clothes, woolen cloths, cattle, sheep, meat, and butter. The world is completely filled with these pleasures, and you offer them.

There are also innumerable varieties, or classes, of offerings, each one filling all space. There are many kinds of offering goddesses, each holding a specific offering. There are heaps of every kind of jewel reaching the sky. There is the multicolored beauty of brocade and so on. There is the melodious sound of cymbals and so on.

Offer all worlds, imagining them filled with offerings. Offer everything you can think of that could be an offering. Offer, without attachment, your own body, possessions, and things. With great devotion that is not just verbal, not just words, with feeling from the depth of your heart, recite sincerely the following prayer:

> Oh! I pray that while I am on this seat, within this very session, upon this very cushion, in this very instant, you will cleanse and purify me of all bad karma and obscurations in my being.
>
> I pray that while I am on this seat, within this very session, upon this very cushion, in this very instant, an exceptional samādhi will arise in me.
>
> I pray that while I am on this seat, within this very session, upon this very cushion, in this very instant, love, compassion, and bodhicitta will arise in me.

Sincerely repeat this prayer over and over again. All the gurus, buddhas, and bodhisattvas—who are assembled in space—become pleased and immediately, simultaneously, say the following words:

> Our sole task is benefitting beings, but we have been unable to, as no one has prayed to us; but now as you, child, have prayed to us, we will give you our blessing.

From the three places of their body, speech, and mind, and from all their pores, countless light rays of blessing and compassion radiate to your body, speech, and mind. Imagine that they completely purify all bad karma and obscurations from your body, speech, and mind, and then pray to them.

So that they will bless you with the power of overwhelming compassion, the buddhas dissolve into the lineage gurus. The lineage gurus, beginning with Vajradhara at the top, dissolve one into the other until they have all dissolved into the root guru. The root guru, the precious master who is the essence of all the buddhas, is brilliant and majestic on the crown of your head, and looks upon you with love and happiness.

Feel intense devotion with great emotion and intense longing. Place your palms together at the heart and—grimacing, choked with inner emotion, your face covered in tears—recite this prayer with intense feeling:

> If children cannot rely on their father, on whom can they
>   rely?
> If children are not protected by their father, who will
>   protect them?
> Give me your blessing right now!

Imagine that your root guru says to you, "Ah, I am a guru worthy of your prayers. Pray to me, my child!" Pray until you shed tears. The main part of the session is spent praying in this way.

When you finish, meditate that the guru completely melts into light and dissolves entirely into your body, so that he blesses you with the power of his overwhelming compassion. You and he blend, and your body and mind rest completely at ease, perfectly relaxed. If no thoughts arise, just rest until they appear. When thoughts do arise, offer a mandala and make the mental offering and supplication described above.

Repeat just this again and again, supplicating with devotion, and when you end, imagine that the guru dissolves into you.

Whether the blessing of the Kagyü lineage enters you or not, whether you develop meditation or not, depends on your devotion. Develop devotion until you shed tears. A dry supplication will bring you only dry blessing, and you will develop only dry meditation. Therefore pray in such a way that you weep.

This alone is the heart of the practice dedicated to devotion. In Dharma terms, it's called the aspect of method. Here it's given the name "preliminaries." It's taught to be the most important of all practices, so dedicate yourself to devotion for half a month.

The instructions for the main practice

> The Conqueror taught that emptiness
> is the samādhi of all the buddhas.
> It can only be attained through the recognition
> of the mind and not through anything else.[49]

From the *Wisdom upon Passing Away Sutra*:

> If the mind is realized, that is wisdom. Therefore meditate perfectly on understanding that buddhahood is not to be searched for elsewhere.[50]

It's called "mind." It's called "knowing." It's called "thoughts." It's called "mindfulness." Essentially it's simply this continuous cognition, this flow of thoughts, that you continually call "my mind." When you know its nature, you attain buddhahood. When you don't know it, you wander in samsara. Therefore you must know the nature of the mind.

This is what the general Dharma teachings call "the aspect of wisdom," but here it's called "the instruction of the main practice." Therefore I earnestly request you to practice it.

As taught above, develop love, compassion, and supreme

bodhicitta; recite the hundred syllables; offer the mandala; supplicate; and so on. It's taught that after completing those:

> Supplicate with intense faith and devotion
> and clearly enter the natural state of your own mind.[51]

And also:

> Without much darkness from examination and analysis,
> relax at ease, resting naturally.[52]

After tears have flowed from genuine devotion to the guru, meditate that the guru, with overwhelming compassion for you, melts into light and dissolves into your body completely. It's taught:

> Merge and deeply, totally relax the body and mind.
> Relax loosely and rest completely. Do not meditate
> on anything. Do not pollute the naturally pure mind
> with the stains of meditation.[53]

Do not meditate on dharmakāya. Do not meditate on transcendence of the intellect. Do not meditate on emptiness. Do not meditate on birthlessness. Do not meditate on luminosity. Do not meditate on mahāmudrā. So what *do* you do?

Do not move the body. Do not close the eyes. Do not go after past consciousnesses. Do not go to meet future consciousnesses. Completely rest solely in the present, without any calculation, but with vivid appearances, clear knowing, and a completely natural, naked consciousness. Rest in a state of clarity and naturalness. Rest relaxed, without tightness. Do not examine or analyze good and bad. Do not have doubts about what is or isn't. When thoughts appear, do not follow after their numerous appearances. Rest completely, like a sheaf of hay that has had its string cut. Rest, relaxed, in natural consciousness. Past thoughts have ceased; the future ones have not arisen. In this relaxed in-between state of the present, it's taught:

> There is no mind in mind; the mind's nature is
> luminosity.[54]

Just this mind alone, which is completely empty, clear, aware, and lucid, is what is called *the perfection of wisdom*, *luminosity*, *mahāmudrā*, *dzokchen*, and *dharmakāya*.

> Look directly and don't be blind!
> Go where you're going and don't wander!
> See the truth and don't obscure it!
> That is the true nature! Rest naturally![55]

With firm control, rest, relaxed and naturally, solely in empty, stainless knowing. It's taught that *meditation* is simply a term used for when, without meditation, you are naturally at rest in simple equanimity. Therefore that is the "meditation" that you should do. That's what's meant by "good practice," and that's what's meant by "essence." Rest in that alone, naturally, as it is, relaxed. If thoughts are not appearing in that state, just rest until they appear. Resting in that way is called "mind" and is called "knowing."

When there is movement, with all kinds of thoughts spontaneously arising, it's taught:

> If you relax this tightly bound mind,
> there is no doubt but that it will be liberated.[56]

Therefore rest, relaxed, on whatever thought arises, whether it is about an external object or the internal mind. When the arising of thoughts ceases, there will be spontaneously the nature of emptiness, without any existence as anything whatsoever. There will be inevitably a perfect clarity, like the center of an autumn's cloudless sky.[57] Don't be glad if it lasts a long time, and don't be upset if it lasts only a short time.

That was a teaching on *mahāmudrā* based on the key point of neither stopping nor creating [thoughts].

When you rest loosely in that way, if the mind is unstable and has strong thoughts, it means you are not free of the wish to meditate. Therefore free yourself from a sense of purpose. Whether the mind is still or not, do not stop anything or create anything.

> A swift mountain river is made pure through its flowing.
> A silver mirror is made clear through being polished.
> A yogin's meditation is made blissful through being
>   destroyed.[58]

Therefore it's taught:

> Rest, relaxed, without meditation.
> If you rest relaxed, the turbidity of this ocean
> of cognition will become clear.[59]

A relaxed mind is all that is necessary. Perfect meditation will arise in a perfectly relaxed mind. A middling meditation will arise in a semirelaxed mind. The least kind of meditation will arise in the least relaxed mind.

Therefore just rest on whatever thought arises. This alone is the root of the instructions, so be firmly fixed upon any spontaneously appearing thought, and relax loosely on it alone. When the next thought appears, rest relaxed in that.

> Meditate in a great number of short sessions.
> When sessions are short, there can be no faults.
> When they are numerous, faults cannot continue.[60]

Therefore relax before a thought arises, before even wishing to give rise to a thought. If you relax like that, it's impossible that this cognition alone will not arise as the dharmakāya. From the *Tantra of the Ocean of Vows*:

> Without contrivance, without distraction, there is spontaneous liberation.
> The spontaneous liberation of appearances is the expanse of great bliss.
> There is just ordinary, fresh relaxation.
> Practice the meditation that is nonmeditation.[61]

When thoughts clearly arise as the dharmakāya, there is no need to eliminate thoughts, and there is no need to create the dharmakāya. Therefore all that you need is just the relaxed mind.

When you are resting in the uncontrived mind, in relaxation, if the mind becomes unstable and manifests thoughts, just leave it alone. Clean and offer a mandala, offering countless mental offerings as described earlier, and just pray with very intense devotion until you're exhausted. Then totally abandon yourself into that state of exhaustion, into the uncontrived mind. If thoughts do not appear, rest completely in that state where there are no thoughts.

If, when you relax and observe in that way, you are destabilized by thoughts, it means that you have lost your mindfulness. You cannot stop thoughts; you cannot eliminate thoughts; you cannot control them; you cannot hold them.

> Do not draw back the mind that moves toward objects,
> but let it be, like a raven that flies from a ship.
> The wise are like cattle herders:
> they let the practicing mind roam freely.[62]

It is said in the *Secret Lamp of Wisdom Tantra*:

> Nondependent, self-illuminating, nongrasping,
> resting nakedly in unimpeded knowing.[63]

If you try to stop thoughts, they keep moving. If you try to hold them, they go away. Therefore let them go to wherever they want without stopping any of them. They won't find anywhere to go. They come naturally, so don't deliberately stop any of them. Don't control any of them. Don't hold on to any of them. Don't deliberately create any of them. Don't contemplate and don't meditate.

When you are simply resting, loose and relaxed, in the uncontrived natural state, thoughts of like or dislike will sometimes arise spontaneously. Look directly at whatever thought arises. Where does it come from? Where is it now? Where does it eventually go? What shape does it have? Is it square? Is it round? Is it triangular? Is it oval? What color is it? Is it white? Is it red? Is it yellow? Is it blue? Is it black? Where is it? Is it on the crown of my head? Is it inside my head? Is it in my upper body? Is it in my limbs? Look to see where it is. Look directly at it to see where it is right now.

It's taught that if you always apply yourself solely to devotion to the guru, resting in an uncontrived state and looking at the mind, this practice will cause the way things truly are to appear from within. Therefore gain complete, utter certainty in which you think, "This nature was here all the time, but until now I was deluded. Now there is no mistake." At that time, this precious mind of yours alone will manifest perfectly as the dharmakāya. Therefore, since you will attain liberation naturally without the need to eliminate thoughts, and since emptiness will naturally arise without the need to cultivate it, you need not seek the dharmadhātu elsewhere. So it has been taught. Thus, since this very variety of thoughts—arising perfectly as the dharmakāya— *is* the true nature, there is no need to meditate with eyes closed;

there's no need to meditate to stop appearances. What the eyes perceive is the union of appearance and emptiness. What the ears perceive is the union of sound and emptiness. The mind is bliss and emptiness. As it is stated:

> The nature of appearances is primordially empty.
> They're not called "empty" because they're destroyed,
>   vanquished, and impermanent.[64]

Forms appear to the eyes, but they are mere appearances without any truly existing essence; that is why they are called the "inseparability of appearance and emptiness." Sounds are heard by the ears, but they are mere sounds with no truly existing nature; that is why they are called the "inseparability of sound and emptiness." Various things appear in the mind, but they have no truly existing nature whatsoever; that is why they are called the "inseparability of knowing and emptiness."

This is what is called "receiving your father's inheritance." It's also called "receiving the blessing of the sacred oral lineage." It's also called "putting the precious jewel in your pocket." It's also called "repaying the guru's kindness." Dedicate yourself to this until it occurs.

First, there is this kind of extensive introduction to the nature of the mind that is repeated over and over. Afterward, there is the main practice's instruction, which is the meaning lineage called "flowing out as buddhahood." The introduction by the guru is no longer necessary, and it arises perfectly within yourself. Therefore have devotion to the guru and rest, relaxed, in the uncontrived mind.

Thus the teaching is simply: "As your own mind is the root of all samsara and nirvana, look to see what it's like."

As a continuation of the teachings of Lord Śākyamuni, Kumāra Candraprabha,[65] the lord of the tenth level,

spread his emanation activity in this land of Tibet.
Thus Dakpo Lhajé came to Daklha Gampo,[66]
led the faithful along the path of devotion,
and had countless accomplished pupils.
Because of his kindness, Tibet became filled with the Dharma.

He entrusted the tradition of this unsurpassable Dharma
to his lineage's countless practicing sons.
Later, the emanated individual, the birthless Shang Gom,[67]
in the presence of the two Buddha statues of Lhasa,[68] and in
    Tsal, and in Gungthang,
taught solely these instructions
to worthy pupils he had gathered through his compassion.
Many became realized, supreme siddhas.

The practice lineage has spread through the kindness of this
    lord.
He is the lama who spread these teachings.
Subsequently, the Shang emanation, the unequaled Dharma
    Lord,
that unrivaled lama,[69] came to the monastery of Pangshong
    Lhari.[70]
He taught nothing but this Dharma
to everyone in his community of pupils,
and every year there was an unceasing appearance of realized
    beings.
This is how he liberated every single one of his pupils.

This is the essence of that lama's practice;
therefore it is superior to all other teachings.

It is the principal teaching of the Kagyüpas;
therefore it is the quintessence of the Dharma, the life essence
    of the ḍākinīs.

I received the lama's teaching again and again.
It remained clear and naked in my mind.
Without forgetting anything, I have written it out correctly,
    without error.
As it is an oral transmission of direct practice instructions,
writing it down could cause its blessing to diminish,
but when done with a pure motivation of respect and love,
without any self-interest, it can't be wrong to do so.

There are great pupils of that lord who by ripening qualities in
    others
have maintained the lineage and cared for the sangha,
but as this is an unmistaken, accurate record of the lama's
    teaching,
it is good that it be preserved and used to teach pupils.

Though I was perfectly seized by the father's hook of
    compassion,
I had no karma of previous practice and little diligence,
so I'm still someone who hasn't developed qualities.
Therefore even this beggar should dedicate himself to this.

I ask for forgiveness from those with eyes of wisdom,
especially from the true guru himself,
for whatever errors there are in what I have written,
and for any faults, such as omitting parts of his speech.

Through the merit of writing this, may all beings throughout
    space,
without exception, practice this Dharma
and manifest within one lifetime
the single quintessence of the equality of the dharmakāya.

I have written, without error, the instructions for the preliminaries and main practice as taught by the precious lama, glorious Lhariwa of the lineage of undiminished blessing.

I, Devakumāra,[71] wrote this at Pangshong Lhari.

Ithi
Maṅgalam

2. The Ultimate Supreme Path of Mahāmudrā

···   ❧❧❧   ···

Lama Shang

Lama Shang Tsöndrü Drakpa (1122–93) is one of the most interest-
ing and also controversial figures in the early history of Tibetan Buddhism.[72] He was already an advanced Kagyü practitioner in the lineage
of Milarepa's pupil Drigom Repa[73] when in 1157—five years after Gampopa's death—he became a pupil of Gampopa's nephew and successor Gomtsul, who was only six years older than Lama Shang.

   Lama Shang founded a monastery at Tsal, near Lhasa, hence the
tradition he founded is named Tsalpa Kagyü. He also inherited Gomtsul's secular responsibilities and established a militia, which he used to
impose his authority over the Lhasa region, which necessitated going
into battle with opposing forces. Lama Shang's successors ruled the
entire Lhasa region for a while, but the Tsalpa Kagyü tradition eventually ceased to have an independent existence.

   Lama Shang is also significant because he is the earliest Kagyüpa
after Gampopa to produce a significant body of literature. He also wrote
a number of biographies and, unusually for Tibet, an autobiography. As
the result of his martial exploits he is not always regarded favorably, but
he is the first of the successive theocracies that would play a dominant
role in Tibetan history. In his *Ultimate Supreme Path of Mahāmudrā*, we
see a wonderful exposition in verse on the nature of the mind.[74]

I PAY HOMAGE to the venerable glorious gurus.

Reverently, I bow to the feet of the realized gurus,
who are the union of infinite, beneficial lassos,[75]
the empowerments that are the ultimate, compassionate
　　activity
of all conquerors throughout the three times.

I will joyfully write, one-pointedly and without error, a repre-
　　sentative fragment
of the innermost essence of all supreme vehicles, the [three]
　　baskets, and the tantras,
which is the mind of all the sugatas,
transmitted from mind to mind by the lords of yogis.

I, Tsöndrü Drakpa, do not have the power to benefit others,
but I have been urged on by my pupils,
who are wise and devoted followers of the Dharma.
I mustn't ignore the faintest possibility of benefit,
so I will write about the mother who gave birth to all conquer-
　　ors and their children,
who is realized by all the trained, worthy ones,
who is the mind treasure of the venerable lineage holders,
who is the essence of all vehicles, scripture, logic, and
　　instruction,
who is the essence of the ultimate, definitive meaning, the
　　dharmakāya,
and who is the naturally pure expanse of luminosity.

1. The View

Whether the conquerors of the three times appear or don't
    appear,
whether the āryas realize it or don't realize it,
whether the buddhas teach it or don't teach it,
whether the commentators explain it or don't explain it,
this pure, elaboration-free luminosity of the true nature
is primordially, naturally present, with neither increase nor
    decrease.

Worlds are formed within pure space and are destroyed
by burning fire, scattering winds, and so on.
Although this destruction occurs throughout many incalcula-
    ble eons,
space remains unharmed, never altered, and neither increases
    nor decreases.

There is darkness when the sun's primordial brightness
is completely obscured by clouds, and there is brightness when
    the clouds vanish.
Despite this apparent increase and decrease,
it is impossible for the sun's essence to increase or decrease.

The unchanging dharmakāya, which is present in the same way,
is nothing other than your own mind.
The entire variety of samsara and nirvana arise in the mind.
The sufferings of the world and its beings arise from the
    confusion
caused by the erroneous delusion of not understanding your
    own mind.

When you have definite understanding of your own mind,
there will be great bliss and the infinite wisdom of nirvana.

Everything manifests from your own mind.
When you recognize the true nature of your mind,
you will know the true nature of all beings.
Knowing that, you will know nirvana and all other
    phenomena.
Knowing all phenomena, you will transcend all three realms.
By knowing one thing, you become wise in all.
By pulling up the roots, the leaves and petals naturally wither.
Therefore gain certainty in the mind alone.

This true nature of the mind, the seed of everything,
primordially identical with the minds of all conquerors and
    their children,
is present as the birthless dharmakāya.

It is immaterial, self-knowing, and self-illuminating.
It is not a thing: it has no color, shape, or size.
It isn't nothing: through conditions, it appears as everything.
It isn't permanent: it is empty by nature.
It isn't nonexistent: its nature is unchanging self-illumination.
It is not a self: when examined, it has no essence.
It is not selfless: it is the great selfhood of freedom from
    elaboration.
It is not the extremes: it has no fixation whatsoever.
It is not the middle way: it is devoid of all dependency.
It cannot be identified by an example's names and symbols.
It has no example: it is like space.
It is not words: it cannot be described by speech.
It is not wordless: it is the cause of all expressions.

It cannot be reached through words such as
existence and nonexistence, truth and falsity,
empty and not empty, peace and no peace,
elaborated and unelaborated,

conceivable and inconceivable,
happiness and suffering, perceivable and unperceivable,
dual and nondual, beyond the intellect and not beyond the
  intellect,
devoid and not devoid, existent and nonexistent,
pure and impure, naturally present and not naturally present.

However profound the words used are,
and however many synonyms are employed,
it is impossible for them to pinpoint the true nature of the mind.

However wise you are, however profound your analysis,
though you describe it for many incalculable eons,
it will be impossible to realize the true nature of the mind,
for its natural condition is not an object for analysis.

However well you try to sieve for
the planets and stars that appear in a lake,
it is impossible to catch a single planet or star,
because those planets and stars are not existent things.

However long you use words to describe it,
no matter what refined terms you use, they are not the true
  nature.
For however long you analyze with your mind,
no matter how profound your understanding, that is not the
  true nature.

As long as there is the duality of seer and seen,
it is impossible to realize the nondual true nature.

In brief, to think that things "are" is the root of attachment to
  everything.
From the root of attachment, all samsara develops.

If you identify by thinking "It's emptiness"
or thinking "It is signless and aspirationless,"
thinking "It is unidentifiable," thinking "It is completely
    pure,"
thinking "It is birthless," thinking "It is unperceivable,"
thinking "It has no nature," thinking "It is without
    elaboration,"
thinking "It is not an object for analysis by speech or mind,"
thinking "It is uncreated and naturally present," and so on,
however profound these thoughts, our recognition of
    emptiness
will not transcend the conceptualization of an arrogant mind.
Attachment to concepts leads to a fall into inferior states
and a continuous ripening of karma from inferior actions.

If the chronic condition of samsara is not cured, the illness will
    continue to occur.
Meditators who have views created by their intellect
remain chronically ill from attachment to sectarianism.
You must have the innate knowledge that is free of thought.

Saying "This is the definitive meaning, the true nature"
is merely conceptual superimposition, a provisional meaning.
There is nothing there that even Śākyamuni could possibly see.
What I'm saying now also cannot describe it.
Know that this is like a finger pointing at the moon.

If you understand this, words and terminology will not
    obscure;
you will be unstained by the faults of words.
Therefore, without abandoning words and analysis,
have no arrogant attachment to their meaning.

The true nature of your own mind

pervades all beings, including their afflictions,
thoughts, aggregates, sensory elements and bases,
and all worlds, including their earth, stones, plants, and trees.

In brief, it pervades everything without exception,
including all inner and outer things.
That pervasion is without the duality of pervader and
    pervaded;
it is the manifestation of one single great identity.

All the planets and stars that appear on a lake
are pervaded by the lake, from which they cannot be separated.
All the waves that move upon the water
are pervaded by water and are inseparable from it.

The movement of mirages in the air
are pervaded by the air and are inseparable from it.

Statues, jewelry, and so on, which are made of gold,
are pervaded by gold and are inseparable from it.

Representations of the six kinds of beings made from molasses
are pervaded by molasses and are inseparable from it.[76]
Space is not separate from a rainbow;
a rainbow is nothing other than space.
The rainbow is space, and space is the rainbow.
They are not separate; they are inseparable and indivisible.

In the same way, the mind and the variety of appearances are
    inseparable.
The mind and emptiness are inseparable;
emptiness and bliss are a great inseparability, a sameness.
In the same way, existence and nirvana are inseparable.

This pervading mind is the mahāmudrā.
Its nature is empty, so there is nothing to be identified.
Its characteristic is clarity—[the mind's] cognition can manifest anything.
Its essence is their inseparability, the union of the vajra mind.
The precious mind is the source of countless qualities.
It is inexhaustible, imperishable, indestructible,
and no one can steal it, this mind that is the treasury of space,
the mind that is as pure as crystal, untarnished by stains.

The mind is like a lamp's flame: it is self-knowing and
  self-illuminating.
The mind has the essence of enlightenment: it has a nature of
  luminosity.
The mind is like a river: it is a constant continuum.
The mind is like space: there is nothing that can be identified.

It is a mind of immaterial wisdom, completely transparent,
like a clean vessel filled with water.

The mind, from which arises all appearances that result from
  propensities,
is like the surface of a polished and unblemished mirror.

2. Separating Samsara from Nirvana

When your own natural mind, present in that way,
is not understood or is misunderstood,
there is the embellishment of conceiving "me" and "mine,"
and these misconceptions cause
afflictions and thoughts to increase.

This accumulates karma, and the ripening of karma causes
the endless suffering of birth, death, and so on,

which are waves on the endless river of samsara,
distracting and disturbing, continuously afflicting.

The myriad propensities for misperceiving
the myriad appearances of the six classes of beings
become established in the mind and multiply thoughts.

Various kinds of bad, errant behavior
cause a continuity of various, unendurable sufferings,
which are experienced over and over again.
These experiences cause stupidity to further increase.
Utterly overcome by ignorance,
the mind is troubled over and over
by anger, pride, desire, miserliness, and the rest.
Oh! Who would put their trust in samsara?

When you realize the true nature of your mind,
the darkness of mistaken views vanishes;
you are liberated from belief in a self, from afflictions and from
    attachment,
and are therefore truly free from all karma and suffering;
the primordially present dharmakāya is revealed,
and the power of your prayers effortlessly accomplishes benefit
    for others.

That which nirvana is dependent upon is so blissful—
a blissful cause, a blissful path, and bliss when there is the
    result!
How frightful are the sufferings of the three realms of
    samsara:
suffering as its cause, path, and result!
So why would you not escape the swamp of samsara
to reach the solid ground of nirvana?

Those who are attracted to nirvana's Dharma,
even the ugly, let alone the good-looking,
will appear beautiful to everyone
as soon as they enter the Dharma,
because their minds have turned toward faith and virtue.

Though you forsake fame, your fame spreads everywhere.
Though you forsake honors, all honor you.
Though you remain humble, all raise you on high.
Though you take on suffering, your life is happy.
Though you are poor, you have plenty of possessions.
Food and clothes effortlessly, spontaneously appear.
Though you flee alone, you meet a host of pupils and
    followers.
Though you do not chase them away, misleaders and hinderers
    flee from you.
Though you do not summon them, deities and Dharma guard-
    ians gather around you.

Even when those who are principally charlatans and frauds,
motivated by attachment, anger, pride, and so on,
do various good activities, such as studying,
it is not a waste, for we can directly see that those people
enjoy the full benefit from those good qualities.

As for those who pretend to be high persons but have little
    learning
and are proud and have the rest of the afflictions,
their outer appearance of a miscellany of good actions
creates an infallible miscellany of good qualities;
thus it is obviously so for a genuine Dharma practitioner.

If such qualities are immediately gained on entering the
    Dharma,

imagine how many qualities come from dedication to its
practice!

In empty valleys and ownerless rocky mountains, .
a conduct that is free of pretense is so spacious!
The happiness that never loses mindfulness is so sublime!
The companionship of deer, who never complain, is so
pleasant!
The clothing and food of pure conduct is warm and beautiful!
The wealth of contentment, free of craving, is inexhaustible!
The armor of patience is so thick and strong!
The powerful, fast steed of diligence is so excellent!
The guru and Jewels, who give blessings, are such an excellent
refuge!
The instructions on the essentials of the path of method are
such a joyful experience!
The samādhi of bliss, clarity, and nonthought is so delicious!
The empty, stainless self-knowing is so bright!
The baseless arising of everything is so hilarious!

Whatever arises never departs from the essential nature, which
is so blissful!
The satisfaction from the nectar of experience is so fulfilling!
Arising from within nonelaboration, the mind is so pure!
Knowing the nature of thought, there is so much certainty!
Gaining mastery over the treasury of knowledge, there is so
much wealth!
Enjoying appearances and beings as the dharmakāya, there is
so much happiness!
Controlling appearances and sounds, there is great power!
Defeating the armies of māras and wrongs views, there is such
wrathfulness!
Escaping from the dungeon of samsara, there is such freedom!

Spontaneously accomplishing the benefit of beings, there is
     great benefit!
Racing across the plain of great bliss, there is such speed!

Even if you spent an eon, you would still not be able
to describe all the qualities that come from diligent practice.
If that is true for the qualities that come from diligent practice,
then it is obviously so for the qualities that come from gaining
     signs of heat.[77]
Even if you spent an eon, you would still not be able
to describe all those qualities, such as miraculous powers and
     clairvoyance.
If that is true for the qualities that come on gaining signs of
     heat,
then it's obviously so for qualities when the three kāyas
     manifest.
It's impossible to ever finish describing the qualities of the
     conquerors,
such as their unsurpassable and inconceivable wisdom.

3. Forsaking Activities

However wise you are in contemplating and analyzing words,
if you do not practice, nothing will arise from within.
It's impossible for intellect's conceptual labeling to realize the
     true nature.
If you do not realize the true nature, it is impossible to purify
     your propensities.
Therefore do not be attached to the academic wisdom of
     words,
but practice the instructions from the guru.
Repeating like a parrot becomes a song of aging and death.
Blind to yourself and others, there is the danger of falling into
     an abyss.

When you are practicing the sacred instructions,
have no attachment to life or body, and forsake activities.
Even if you are hungry, cold, sick, or dying from starvation,
forsake everything, for it is just a dream.

Even if everyone reviles you and you acquire a bad reputation,
be humble and dedicate yourself to the essence of practice.

The fear of death from cold and hunger
is a cause for not abandoning worldly activities.
The few qualities that this beggar monk Shang has
are the benefit of using my life and body like targets.

Even if you have abandoned all wealth, right down to a needle
    and thread,
if you worry about supporting yourself, you are not a
    renunciate.
If you don't reject the wish to avoid what is unpleasant,
there will never be a time when you abandon worldly
    activities.

If you do not banish the entire world from your mind,
even though you can be generous, maintain conduct,
make offerings to the guru, remain in solitude,
dedicate yourself to meditation, have good experiences,
have great wisdom, have high realization,
or perform any good action, you will just be meaninglessly
    tiring yourself.

If you don't understand how to banish the world from your
    mind
and you don't even wish for the happiness of the devas,
it's obvious that you must be aspiring for happiness in this life.

As long as thoughts have not ceased,
it's impossible to avoid preoccupation with future days.
Therefore cast everything aside, become a devotee of the sacred.
Devote yourself to the treasury of instructions,
be unaffected by the armies of outer and inner māras,
and maintain a pure conduct whether in public or in private.

If you can do this by yourself, then wander alone in the
    mountains.
Maintain a pure conduct, free of pretense.
Have a motivation to benefit others, free of bias and
    attachment.
Develop the aspiration for enlightenment for the sake of all
    beings.
Apply yourself to genuine practice that is neither too tight nor
    too loose.

Practice the instructions just as they have been taught,
without focusing the mind on any happiness or unhappiness,
such as threats to life, heat and cold, hunger and thirst,
and without becoming seduced by fame and material wealth.

4. The Different Classes of Individuals and the Gradualist Path

Beings have an inconceivable variety of conducts,
and all their individual capabilities are countless.
Because of the different levels of their training,
the teachings of the conquerors are endless.

Summarizing them, the teachings are of three kinds,
which accord with different levels of training:
there are individuals who are gradualist,
those who are immediate, and those who are nonsequential.

The perfect path for a gradualist
would be an inappropriate Dharma for an immediate.
The perfect path for an immediate
would be an inappropriate Dharma for gradualists.

The perfect food for the peacock is aconite,[78]
but if others eat it they will die.
The perfect dwelling place for fish is water,
but humans and others drown in it,
while fish die if they are on dry land.

That which heals a hot illness
is harmful for someone with a cold illness.
That which is good for someone with a cold illness
is very harmful for someone with a hot illness.

Thus different vehicles are taught
to the same individual at different levels.
That which is beneficial at an earlier level
is bondage at a higher level.
That which is beneficial at a higher level
is a cause of downfall at a lower level.

A cooling potion is beneficial
at the onset of a hot illness,
but is very harmful while recovering from it.

Therefore know that there are different phases
and different levels of capabilities,
such that different paths should not malign each other.

The individuals who are gradualists should first
contemplate the difficulty of obtaining a precious human
    existence,

become saddened by the terrors of the lower existences,
contemplate the impermanence of the precious human
     existence,
and quickly go for refuge in the Three Jewels.

They should then take the eight one-day vows
and then the five lifetime vows
and the successive training of the novice monk and fully
     ordained monk.

They should turn away from the phenomena of samsara,
have their minds fixed on nirvana,
keep the discipline of striving for liberation,
and learn the philosophies of the Vaibhāṣikas and
     Sautrāntikas.

Then, in order to reject the lesser enlightenment,
they should meditate on repaying the kindness of beings,
become habituated to love and compassion,
and develop the aspiration to supreme enlightenment.

In the three phases of preparation, main part, and conclusion,
they should practice the six perfections
and gather the two accumulations.
Uniting emptiness and compassion,
they should become familiarized with stability and insight,
training well their own beings.

They should dedicate themselves continuously to the benefit
     of others
with an altruistic motivation free of self-interest.

An individual who has trained in that way
should then enter the Vajrayāna

and train in the four tantras in sequence
in order to accomplish the kāya with seven aspects.[79]

Those in the highest yoga tantras
should receive the vase empowerment,
keep their commitments properly,
and train in the generation stage.

Then they should receive the secret empowerment
and bless themselves with the power of the channels and
    winds.

Then they should meditate on the bliss and emptiness of the
    third empowerment
and become familiar with the ultimate fourth
    empowerment.

I have specifically described the gradualist individual,
but there are countless classes of individuals:
there are those who must progress through the vehicles from
    the beginning,
there are those for whom a rough training will suffice,
and there are those who have no need to train.

There are those who obtain the empowerment without
    receiving it,
there are very many who have not obtained the empowerment
    even though they have received it,
there are those who have both received and obtained the
    empowerment,
there are those who have neither received nor obtained it,
there are those who have the primordial possession of the
    empowerment.

Therefore, with the knowledge of what kind of individual the
    pupil is,
the pupil should practice accordingly.

5. *The Method of Meditation*

I, Tsöndrü Drakpa, on the urging of my pupils,
who are wise and devoted followers of the Dharma,
and not wanting to ignore the slightest chance of being
    beneficial,
will explain the training that worthy ones should
    understand.

The immediate kind of individuals
should please the guru of the lineage
with their bodies and every possession.

They should receive empowerment and blessing
and, uplifted by the bodhicitta
together with the practice of a deity,
meditate from the very beginning
on the definitive meaning: the mahāmudrā.

A guru who has the quintessence of realization
directly introduces them to the wisdom they already have,
as if it were a treasure in their own hands.
They should remain, without distraction, in a state of
    nonmeditation,
where there is neither meditator nor anything on which to
    meditate.

The desire for numerous complexities
obscures the naturally present wisdom.
There is no need for a precise plan of action

in the meditation of mahāmudrā;
it does not have the stages of preliminaries, a main part,
and a conclusion, nor does it have any definitive numbers;
there is no need to calculate times and dates.
Whenever one has mindfulness, rest with relaxation.

Your mind is birthless and continuous,
without a beginning, middle, or end.

The rising and sinking of agitated waves
ceases by itself without interference.
This mind that is obscured by thoughts,
when left as it is, unmodified, will clarify as the dharmakāya.

Do not modify it, but rest in relaxation.
Do not control the mind, but let it go free.
Do not have intentions, but be spacious.
Do not focus on anything, but be expansive.
Do not be overactive, but rest in stillness.
Do not seek out somewhere to rest the mind;
rest without any basis, like space.

Keep the mind fresh, without thinking
of the past, the future, or the present.
Whether thoughts are appearing or not,
do not purposefully meditate, but rest naturally.

In brief, do not meditate on anything,
but let the mind go wherever it wants.

There is no need to be afraid of anything:
you will never depart from the dharmakāya.
Just by allowing the mind to relax
there will be an experience of clarity and nonthought,

and you will rest as if in the center of pure space:
this is the luminosity, the dharmakāya.

When a thought instantly springs from
that resting state,
do not think of it as something that is
other than the luminosity, the dharmakāya.
It is the same as when waves rise
from a clear, still sea
and are nothing other
than that clear sea.

The mind is the basis of thoughts.
Clarity and knowing are the characteristics of the mind.
Emptiness is the nature of that clarity and knowing.
Great bliss is the essence of emptiness.

The darkness of concepts has never existed
within the nature of the mind,
and so it is named *luminosity*.
Its knowing and emptiness are inseparable,
And therefore it is named *union*.

The nature of all phenomena
is the essence of the mind's knowing.
The essence of the mind's knowing
has no body with features;
it is a bodiless body, which is the supreme body.

Bodilessness is the body of the true nature (*dharmatā*),
and therefore it is named the truth body (*dharmakāya*).

Therefore the appearance of a thought
is emptiness appearing from emptiness,

the dharmakāya appearing from the dharmakāya,
luminosity appearing from luminosity,
union appearing from union,
the dharmadhātu appearing from the dharmadhātu,
purity appearing from purity,
Vajrasattva appearing from Vajrasattva,
enlightenment appearing from enlightenment.

Ignorant persons, who have no propensities from previous
    training
and have not obtained the true instructions,
make a distinction between the appearance
and the nonappearance of thoughts,
between thought and nonthought,
and between the mind and the dharmakāya.

They see thoughts as faults and stop them.
They wish for nonthought and deliberately create it,
but the wandering waves keep on moving.

The nonthought created by stopping thought
is thought. It is a delusion.
It is a great darkness that obscures the dharmakāya.

Those who do not wish to give rise to thought
are those who wish to remain in nonthought.
That desire leads to becoming a *gongpo* demon
and exhausts the treasury of natural wealth.
Meditators who stop their thoughts
are like people churning water for butter:
they will not see any benefit,
even if they meditate for an eon.

Therefore it's unnecessary to stop thoughts.

If they've stopped, there is no need to create them.
Though they appear, the dharmakāya is also present,
for they do not depart from the dharmakāya.

If you have the instructions from a sublime guru,
when there is movement there is liberation,
and when there is stillness there is liberation.
Without instructions from a sublime guru,
when there is movement there is bondage,
and when there is stillness there is bondage.

Therefore you must receive the instructions.
Be certain that thoughts arise as your friends.
Refrain from preoccupying yourself with much analysis.
Instead relax freely and be naturally at rest.

Do not follow after externals
but let the mind go wherever it wants.

Do not look at external objects.
Do not even look at your own mind.

The objects are empty and the mind too is empty.
There is no need to feel afraid.

If you think "this is it,"
that will plant the seed of attachment to an object.
If the seedling of conceit appears,
it will grow into the tree of samsara.

Do not obscure the mind with the darkness of meditation,
for the mind is primordially pure and luminous,
and meditation will destroy the effortless result.

Do not stir up the turbidity of desire
in the clear sea of the mind,
for that will obscure the jewels of the dharmakāya.

Do not smear the stains of meditation
upon the unblemished mirror of the mind,
for then you will not see the reflection of wisdom.

Do not use the clay of concepts to cover up
the precious jewel of the mind,
for that will prevent the desired and required result.

In brief, rest the mind without thinking "this is it!"
Rest the mind without thinking "this isn't it!"
The mind's thoughts of "is" and the mind's thoughts of "isn't"
are two mutually dependent fixations.
If there is absolutely no "is" at all,
then there will be absolutely no "isn't" at all.

Let go completely in a state free from thinking.
Don't think of "resting" or "not resting."
Don't think of "letting go" or "not letting go."
Don't even think "think!" or "don't think!"

Whether you are moving, sitting, or standing,
whether you are meditating, sleeping, or eating,
whether you are talking, sleeping, or anything,
it's essential that it be done with the natural mind.

6. Experience

Rest your own mind, this naturally present dharmakāya,
as it is, without modification,
and specific experiences will happen.

There are three kinds: those of the gradualist,
the indeterminate, and the immediate.

The way that experiences happen for gradualists:
At first there is simply resting,
then experiences definitely happen,
and then clear realization arises.

When there is the first state of resting,
thoughts arise uninterruptedly,
like water rushing down a cliff.
So you think, "Am I not able to meditate?"

The experience of this amount of thoughts arising
is the result of the mind being able to rest a little.
Before you rested in this way,
thoughts arose as they wished,
and you were not aware of the procession of thoughts.

Next the mind slows and thoughts diminish,
becoming like a slowly moving river.

Then the mind will rest, immovable and stable,
like the depths of the ocean.

Then there will come experiences:
experiences of clarity, nonthought, and bliss,
like the center of pure space.
There is undistracted self-illumination,
like a lamp's flame undisturbed by wind.
There is lucidity, vividness, and ease,
like a rainfall of beautiful flowers.
There is brightness, evenness, and insubstantiality,
like the sun shining in a cloudless sky.

There is transparency and purity,
like a bronze vessel filled with water.

There is no end to words such as these.
They have no basis, appearing like dreams.
They are insubstantial, appearing like rainbows.
They are ungraspable, appearing like the moon on water.
It is like enjoying the pleasures of space—
everything is experienced but is experienced as nothing.

This nonexperience is the supreme experience.
All experiences have gone away.
Within nonexperience, there is nothing to be freed from.

7. Nondual Realization

When you have those kinds of experiences,
realization's wisdom clearly arises.
If realization's wisdom doesn't arise,
however excellent those experiences may be,
they're like cutting down a tree but not touching the roots,
so that the agony of the afflictions will still grow.

Therefore the arising of realization is crucial.
The arising of the wisdom of realization
certainly does not happen through desire,
it does not come through skill in analysis,
it does not come through great learning,
and it is beyond the scope of academics.

The nonthought created by stopping thought,
however deep and strong it may be,
is a great obscuration that prevents the birth of wisdom.

The spontaneous arising of realization's wisdom
certainly does not come
through desire or acquisition,
through being skilled or unskilled in analysis,
through great or little learning,
through wisdom or stupidity,
through good or bad experiences,
through intense or weak efforts, and so on.
It comes through relying upon a guru
and through your own merit.

"Relying upon a guru" means that
you receive it by pleasing a realized guru.
"Through your own merit" means that wisdom
comes to those predisposed through former training.

Therefore, as the wisdom of realization
is acquired on the path of blessing,
it is experienced by those who have faith,
it arises within those who have veneration,
and it is realized by those who are trained.
Diligence is an aid in all of these.
It is the worthy ones with the highest capability who see wisdom.
The minds of those skilled only in words can't comprehend it.

The nondual realization that worthy individuals have
comes through the blessing of a sublime guru:
the dharmakāya arises from the middle of realization,
nonduality arises from the middle of the mind,
wisdom arises from the middle of the afflictions,
and realization arises from the middle of experiences.

The delusion of dualism will completely vanish,
as when a sleeping man wakes up.

On meeting nondual wisdom you awake and think,
"Oh! It's been here all along,
but I hadn't realized it!
Nondual wisdom: what a joy!
My previous conduct: so shameful!
It's realizing and not realizing it
that differentiates samsara from nirvana.
Up until now, before this realization,
I was like a man who was just
asleep and dreaming dreams:
I dreamed that I wandered in the ocean of samsara.
I dreamed that I suffered in the hells and so on.
I dreamed that, troubled, I turned to the guru.
I dreamed that I practiced his instructions.
I dreamed that experiences arose in my mind.
I dreamed that the luminosity arose as the dharmakāya.
I dreamed that the darkness of thought was dispelled.
I dreamed that there was no separation between meditation
    and post-meditation.
I dreamed that realization arose.
I dreamed that objectless compassion arose
toward beings without realization.
I dreamed that I attained the supreme mahāmudrā
and that my form kāyas spontaneously accomplished the ben-
    efit of beings."

When you suddenly wake from that sleep,
there was no suffering of samsara,
there was no turning to the guru because you were troubled,
there was no practicing his instructions,
there was no arising of experiences in the mind,
there was no arising of luminosity as the dharmakāya,
there was no dispelling the darkness of thoughts,
there was no remaining in nonthought,

there was no arising of wisdom's realization,
there was neither beings nor compassion,
there was neither enlightenment nor attainment,
there was neither beings nor benefiting them,
there was neither truth nor falsity.
They were nothing but dream appearances.

Where did the samsara that you dreamed of
come from and where did it go?
Where did nirvana, the elimination of samsara,
come from and where did it go?
They and everything else were dream phenomena.
Where did they come from and where did they go?

It is the same as when a great king,
without leaving his throne for an instant,
in an illusion sits on a horse that runs away,
crossing many mountain passes and valleys.
Many months and years go by,
and he experiences all kinds of happiness and sorrow,
all without ever leaving his throne
and without even the morning having passed by.

In the instant when realization arises,
when there is that great wisdom,
you comprehend the nature of all phenomena,
without becoming conceited by thinking "I comprehend."
The nondual wisdom becomes manifest,
yet you don't become conceited by thinking "It has manifested
    to me."
You are liberated from the three realms and from the Lesser
    Vehicle,
yet you don't become conceited by thinking "I'm liberated."

In the instant that you realize nonduality,
you have certainty that all appearances and sounds are mind,
so that the Aspectarian[80] doctrine is made manifest.
You have certainty in the clarity of the mind,
so that the Non-Aspectarian[81] doctrine is made manifest.
You know self-knowing to be like an illusion,
so that the Illusion[82] doctrine is perfected.
You know illusion to be empty,
so that the Utterly Nonabiding[83] doctrine is perfected.

Emptiness arises as bliss
so that the view of nondual union is perfected.
That union has nonattention,
so that the mahāmudrā is made manifest
but without any identification through thinking "It has
      manifested."

This wisdom through realization
does not come from anywhere,
does not go anywhere,
and does not reside anywhere.

The wisdom of realization and what it realizes
both dissolve into the nonconceptual essence of
      phenomena
without the arrogance of identifying it as the essence.

Now remain within the equality that is like space.
Truly look at that which is true
and makes all thought and words meaningless.
When you truly see, you will be liberated.

The children have become tired
of the games that I have played.

If there is anything, offer it to the guru.
If there isn't anything, let the mind relax.

That is the gradualist's process of development.

In the indeterminates' process of development,
they gain stability, experiences, and realization.
An exceptional realization may arise first,
but that realization will be unstable, like waves.
They may sometimes have experiences and
sometimes have stability, in no certain order.
They are able to have both higher and lower experiences.

For the immediate kind of individuals,
experience, realization, and stability
arise simultaneously, without meditation,
as soon as a guru, who has the essence of realization,
teaches the instructions to them
or just by looking at their own minds.

Whether their experiences increase or decrease,
their realization remains unchanged,
just as a tree remains unchanged
even though a monkey climbs up and down it;
just as the sky remains unchanged
even though rainbows appear or disappear in it;
just as the depths of the ocean do not change
whether waves rise or cease upon its surface.
It doesn't matter what experiences come or go
in the mind that is the natural presence of the
    dharmakāya.

If those who have clear experiences
do not blend those experiences with realization,

they will be like lamp flames in a tempest,
which will be ruinous for beginners.

For meditators who have gained stability,
everything, whether good or bad, will be an aid.
So beginners, don't try to compete.

When a lamp is tiny,
even a faint breeze extinguishes it.
When a great fire blazes in a forest,
a strong wind merely fans the flames.

Meditators who don't have stability
may have occasional realizations,
but they have to feed the torch of realization
with the dry wood of experiences,
while too much damp wood will extinguish it.

However high your realizations,
if your stability and experiences are not stable,
if you have no control over your own mind,
the afflictions—your enemies—will capture you.

That is like when an important man,
seized by enemies and held captive by weapons,
is on the road that leads home
but is not free to follow it.

Therefore it's essential to maintain the torch
    of realization
through having stable experiences.
If you don't have control over your own mind,
you will lose the confidence of realization.

It's not in the mouth of someone who's all talk.
Be careful all you meditators,
for talking counteracts experiences.

8. Conduct

For practitioners of mahāmudrā,
the colors of experiences appear
in the wish-fulfilling jewel of realization,
and needs and desires are fulfilled through their conduct.

When individuals who are gradualists
enter onto the Mantrayāna path,
they keep far from negative thoughts
and wish to be free from samsara.

Their minds are fixed upon great enlightenment,
and with motivation devoid of self-interest,
they develop the bodhicitta to benefit beings.

They always have the pride of being the deity;
they repeat mantras, recite, and offer mandalas and
    tormas;
they practice the seven branches, such as offerings;[84]
they make a gift of tormas to pretas;
and they offer water and medicine to the nāgas.

With their possessions, they honor and serve the guru,
provide feasts for the sangha, hold *gaṇacakras*,[85]
give to beggars without reservation,
perform the outer and inner *homa* fire rituals,[86]
creates *tsatsas*,[87] stupas, and statues,
save the lives of animals, and chant the canon.

In brief, in between the generation and completion practice
    sessions,
they do nothing but good actions
with a motivation of great compassion,
never remaining in neutral activity,
let alone engaging in bad conduct.

They behave like venerable monks
or just like new brides:
maintaining careful conduct,
their actions all conforming to goodness.

They purify their outer and inner obscurations
and are dedicated to the accumulation of merit.
They keep their good qualities secret, augmenting them privately.

Those who ignore karma
and malign relative methods
are like birds without wings;
they will certainly fall into the abyss of lower existences.
Therefore avoid even the smallest bad action,
and practice even the smallest good action.

Those who have continuous diligence
in the practice of good actions
gain a small degree of stability
and distinguish between outer and inner conduct.

Their public conduct accords with other beings.
In solitude, they develop the inner conduct of samādhi.
When they increase the experience of inner conduct,
they adopt a conduct that accords with that experience,
which then increases their samādhis and realizations—
something beginners cannot experience.

They practice with the five nectars[88]
and depend upon the five powers.[89]
They do not give up the five sensory pleasures
but give up attachment to them and use them as aids.

Water and compost cause
rice sprouts to grow in the fields.
Reliance on sensory pleasures causes
the sprouts of practice's wisdom to grow.

In their conduct they have no attachment to anything
because they have the continuous experience of birthlessness.
This relaxed natural conduct of the six consciousnesses
is accompanied by the realization of nonduality.

They perform any conduct they wish
without discriminating between what should and should not
     be done.

Experiencing the realization of nonduality,
they wear anything, good or bad,
without thinking about which clothes can be worn and
     which not.

Without thinking about which food can be eaten and
     which not,
they eat anything, pure or impure,
and nonconceptual wisdom increases.

Without thinking about what can be said and what can't,
they just say whatever comes to mind.

They do not deliberately do anything.
They remain in a natural state of relaxation.

They are never apart from the experience of the dharmakāya.
They have no attachment to anything.

They are not disturbed, even for an instant,
by any good or bad thing
their own followers or others do
but remain as unresponsive as matter.

They never perform
activities that are harmful to the mind.
They flee from humans,
just like deer flee from humans.

They do not argue about whether others are good or bad
while proudly thinking of themselves as good.
They always conceal their qualities,
just like swindlers keep their faults secret.

They do not talk big like an important man
but always remain humble.
Even if they have realized every level of meaning,
they always make offerings to the gurus and ḍākinīs.

In brief, they abandon all self-interest,
deception, and artifice.

For as long as there is a meditation and post-meditation,
they examine to see if their minds
are stable or unstable in meditation.
If the mind in meditation is unstable,
it's pointless to practice a stupid meditation
within a state of dullness and obscurity.
Instead they dedicate their body and speech
to good actions motivated by love and compassion.

However, when meditation is stable,
even if it means desisting from good conduct by body and
    speech,
they apply themselves solely to becoming adept in meditation.

Meditation and *post-meditation*
don't mean "sitting down" and "standing up."

The beginners' meditation
is unwavering one-pointedness
upon any positive object whatsoever;
whether sitting or moving around, it's meditation.
If they don't remain one-pointed
and become lost in thought,
though they meditate on a cushion, it's post-meditation.

The meditation of realizing your own mind
is known as the successive four yogas.

The *one-pointed yoga* arises
when you realize the characteristics of your own mind
as unceasing emptiness and clarity, without center or periphery,
like the middle of pure space.
That pure and vivid state
is the meditation of the first yoga.

When thoughts arise within that state,
even if you're meditating on a cushion, it's post-meditation.
If you remain in that pure, vivid clarity and emptiness,
whether you're talking, moving, or sitting,
you remain in the state of meditation.

The *yoga of nonelaboration* arises
when you realize the essence of your own mind

75

as a continuity of knowing, free from conceptual elaboration,
in which your own mind is the dharmakāya,
without birth or cessation, adoption or rejection.
That is the meditation of the second yoga.

When you remain in that meditation,
whether you're moving, sitting, or talking,
you remain in the state of meditation.
If you become distracted by the elaboration of concepts,
even if you're meditating on a cushion, it's post-meditation.

The *yoga of one taste* arises
when you realize the character of your own mind,
when you realize that the multiplicity of samsara and nirvana
arises from your mind, which is the dharmakāya free from
    conceptual elaboration.

The entire array of thought and nonthought,
appearances and no appearance, resting and no resting,
empty and not empty, clarity and no clarity,
are all one taste in the luminosity of the dharmakāya.

You don't see any appearances that are not the dharmakāya.
You don't see any thought that is not luminosity.

When the mind has that realization of one taste,
it is the meditation of the third yoga.

While there is that natural mind,
whether you're running, jumping, or talking,
you remain in the state of meditation.
When you don't have the natural mind,
even if you're meditating on a cushion, it's post-meditation.

The *yoga of nonmeditation* arises
when the nature of knowing has no basis.
The practitioner has nothing to meditate on;
there is no meditator, only a state of evenness.

You will know what is meant by
"Buddhahood, with its three kāyas
and five wisdoms, is complete in me."
You will have complete certainty that this itself
is the accomplishment of mahāmudrā.
You will not be conceited, thinking,
"I have attained the primordially present accomplishment!"
There will be neither mindfulness nor the absence of
    mindfulness.
There will be neither attention nor nonattention.
There will be neither one taste nor the absence of
    one taste.

There are no stages of meditation and post-meditation
in that self-sustaining knowledge of nonduality.
There is no death and there is no birth
in the continuous presence of knowing and emptiness.

A garuḍa's powers are already complete within the egg;
as soon as it hatches, it flies into the sky.
The qualities of the three kāyas are already complete within
    the mind;
as soon as the body's trap is destroyed, they will benefit
    others.
When this nonmeditation arises,
there are no stages of meditation and post-meditation.

However high your realization,
while you are still familiarizing yourself with it,

there will still be stages of meditation and post-meditation,
there will still be mindfulness and the absence of mindfulness,
and there will still be distraction and the absence of
  distraction.

When you have completed the process of familiarization,
that is called *nonmeditation*,
where there are no stages of meditation and post-meditation,
there is nothing but a continuous state of meditation.
The mind of natural realization is present,
so whether you are moving about, sitting, or lying down,
whether you are sleeping or dreaming,
whether you are talking or eating,
there is nothing but meditation.

It is the jewel that naturally fulfills all needs and wishes.
It is the sun that naturally has light.
It is the yoga of constant meditation.
It is called *manifest nonduality*.

In the post-meditation of one-pointedness,
things appear to be solid
but are meditated upon as illusions.

In the post-meditation of nonelaboration,
things sometimes appear as illusions
and sometimes they appear to be solid,
but they are meditated upon as the dharmakāya.

In the post-meditation of the one-taste phase,
things arise as the dharmakāya when there is mindfulness,
but there are brief periods of solidity, when there is no
  mindfulness.

In nonmeditation, both meditation
and post-meditation are nothing but the dharmakāya,
and the two form kāyas appear to others.

It's not in the mouth of someone who's all talk.
It's not in a mouth that boasts empty words.
Don't keep yourself in the dark![90]

When there is nonmeditation,
whether you are asleep or not, there is clarity.
Whether you are analyzing or not,
whether you have mindfulness or not,
there is clearly the dharmakāya, with no self or others.
Without any thought of making an effort,
objectless compassion arises spontaneously.

Until you reach that level,
you are in grave danger of deceiving yourself
with a nonmeditation that's just clinging to empty talk.

Therefore, worthy meditators,
until you reach the level of nonmeditation,
honor the guru and accumulate merit.
If you are not deceived by clinging to empty talk,
your accumulation of merit will never let you down.
That is the heart advice of the realized ones.

As for being with others or being in solitude,
if you always have the wisdom of the dharmakāya,
are free from attachment to duality,
and are not overcome by the eight worldly concerns,
you will always be in solitude, even though you wander
    through a crowd.
However, if you have attachment to duality,

have ups and downs, and so on,
you are always in a crowd, even when you're in solitude.
Therefore, whether in solitude or with others,
always have the realization of nonduality,
don't go through ups and downs,
and prize having no attachment to anything.

The distinctions between solitude and company,
between meditation and post-meditation, and so on
are taught with the intention of guiding
those individuals who are beginners.
Ultimately there are no such dualities
as solitude and company, meditation and post-meditation.

Why is that? Because the mind
is the innate dharmakāya,
and appearances are the innate light of the dharmakāya,
just like a lamp's flame and its light.

Dharmakāya is the nature of knowing;
it can't possibly have discontinuity or fluctuation.
So how could there be meditation and post-meditation?
Who can deny the absence of meditation and post-meditation
in a meditator who has this enduring realization?
That is why they cannot be judged like ordinary individuals.

You may have experiences or realizations and think you are special,
but no matter how good the experiences are,
liberation is impossible without realization;
no matter how high the realizations are,
without compassion, they will be the śrāvaka path.

Even if you have experiences and samādhis
within the four dhyānas and so on,

if you have the great fault of being without realization,
those experiences will cease, and afterward
you will fall into the three lower existences and so on
and experience unendurable suffering; think about that!

All experiences are composite;
everything composite is impermanent and will end.
Therefore have no attachment to experiences
and realize nondual wisdom.

This nonabiding nirvana
is solely the province of realization.
Mentally fabricated nonduality,
which is what great scholars realize,
is solely the province of thought.

The nonduality that arises within
is nothing but the blessing of the guru.
The faithful who have veneration for the guru
develop the certainty of realization within themselves.
What does someone who just analyzes have?
Even I have understood it as words, too.

When realization arises in your mind,
examine to see whether it can withstand negative factors.
If someone on your right is swinging an axe at you
and saying all kinds of unpleasant things to you
while someone on your left offers you the aroma of
      sandalwood
and respectfully says all kinds of pleasant thing to you,
if while you're having this experience,
you have no happiness or suffering, no like or dislike,
without having to make an effort to cope with it,
then you're ready to perform crazy behavior in public.

However, if you have no faith or if it's unstable,
if you haven't gained unimpeded powers,
and you publicly carry out the secretly taught conduct,
you will bring yourself and others to ruin.

When you have gained unimpeded powers,
such as various kinds of clairvoyance,
some of which may possibly be of benefit to others,
don't distinguish between secret and public conduct.

The venerable Mila taught that
the ten virtuous actions are not to be performed,
that the ten bad actions are not be abandoned,
and that you should rest in natural relaxation.

Venerable Loro[91] taught that
the powerful, high Three Jewels
are completely present in a state of devotionless knowing
in which there is nothing that can be called "going for refuge."

These viewpoints of those venerable ones
are as clear as a butter lamp in a bowl
to me, the beggar monk from Shang,
and to all my realized vajra siblings.

But if I explain it, you will find it hard to understand,
for it's experienced only by those in whom it has sponta-
    neously arisen,
by those who have faith, by those who have pleased their gurus
and whose blessing has entered into their hearts.

I am not going to describe the "all-victorious" conduct,
the "great meditation" conduct, or any of the others,[92]
as I think that it would take too long;

since you can read about them within the ocean of supreme
    tantras,
I don't have to write too much here.

Perform the appropriate conduct at the appropriate time.
Avoid senseless behavior and empty chatter.
Practice without being too tight or too loose.
Maintain a view that is free of partiality.
Have a conduct that is free of artifice.
Have compassion that is without bias.
Meditate free from distraction.
Then there will be unceasing good qualities
and the accomplishment of unending benefit for beings.

If, without the realization of nonduality,
you could be liberated by
deliberately senseless behavior—
regarding enemies and friends, gold and clods of earth, as the
    same,
and having no regard for respectability or reputation—
then why don't little children become liberated?

If, without the realization of nonduality,
you could be liberated by disregard for what is proper,
then every lunatic would be liberated.

If, without the realization of nonduality,
you could be liberated by disregard for cleanliness,
then every dog and pig would be liberated.

If, without the realization of nonduality,
you could be liberated by skillful conduct,
then every new bride would be liberated.

If you could be liberated by a natural relaxation
that lacks the realization of nonduality,
then every idiot would be liberated.

If you do have the realization of nonduality,
then however you act, whether wild or precise, you will be
    liberated.
If you don't have the realization of nonduality,
whether your conduct is precise or wild, you will be in bondage.

If you are permeated by impartial compassion,
whatever you do will be the supreme path.
If you are not permeated by impartial compassion,
whatever you do will be the inferior path.

9. The Commitments

How do you keep the commitments?

When you are on the level of a beginner,
do not break the pratimokṣa vows
or other commandments of the Sugata and gurus.

When you are at the level of meditating on channels and
    winds,
avoid anything that is contrary to bliss and heat.

When the experience of nonthought arises,
avoid anything that is contrary to samādhi.
When you have seen the essence of your own mind,
avoid anything that is harmful to the mind.

When the realization of nonduality has arisen,
avoid all goal-oriented action.

Make your own mind the judge of everything.
When the meaning you realize is always the true nature,
then there is no commitment to keep, and that is the supreme
    commitment.
That is what is called the *white panacea*.[93]

10. The Result

If you have a view that is unmistaken,
receive instructions that are appropriate and correct;
meditate without error, neither too tight nor too loose;
have conduct free of attachment, unstained by faults;
and keep your commitments without feeling shame before the
    deities.
Then you will without doubt gain the necessary desired
    results.

It is like the example of a medicinal tree:
When the ground, seed, time, water, compost,
and all the correct factors for the dependent origination of the
    result are present,
then even the seedling will be able to cure illness.
Therefore the entire trunk, branches,
leaves, flowers, and fruits
with their complete qualities
will heal all illness.

If negative factors of dependent origination
have the power to result in suffering,
then good, unmistaken factors
will obviously bring excellent happiness.

If composite dualism's factors of dependent origination
result in happiness and suffering,

then the nondependent, the noncomposite, the inconceivable
will obviously result in infinite wisdom.

If virtuous actions performed with attachment to reality
result in happiness in the higher existences,
then objectless, nonconceptual virtue
will obviously result in buddhahood.

If bliss, clarity, and nonthought accompanied by attachment
result in the bliss of devas within the three realms,
then bliss, clarity, and nonthought that is free from attachment
will obviously result in attaining the three kāyas of the
    conquerors.

If emptiness without method and wisdom
results in the bliss of the śrāvakas and pratyekabuddhas,
then the inseparability of emptiness and compassion
will obviously result in the location-free great bliss.

Ideally, beginners with the correct practice
of meditation and post-meditation in the generation stage
will cause the perfect union—the saṃbhogakāya—
to manifest within their lifetime
or, otherwise, to manifest in the bardo.[94]
Otherwise, they will definitely attain the perfect good fortune
of a deva's existence in the next life,
where they will then manifest the union, the saṃbhogakāya.
If they are reborn as humans,
they will accomplish it within seven lifetimes.

The medium result is that when experiences arise
in the completion stage with attributes,
they will instantly purify a great mass of bad karma,
and the dākiṇīs will bestow their blessings on them.

Familiarization with the experiences
of bliss, clarity, and nonthought will definitely result in realization,
so that the three kāyas will definitely manifest in their lifetime
or at least will definitely manifest in the bardo.

Even if the realization of nonduality does not arise
in practitioners of great diligence
who have received the profound instructions,
they will truly attain transference of consciousness,
either through entering into another's body
or through an upward transference of consciousness.
If they fail to do that, they will appear in the bardo,
where the best will manifest the luminosity,
the medium will accomplish the illusory body of union,
and the least will close the entrance to the city of the womb
or will control where they will be reborn,
after which the three kāyas will doubtless manifest.

When the mahāmudrā yogins
loosely relax their minds,
an experience of clarity without thought—
like the center of pure space—arises.

At the very moment when that arises,
countless bad karmas and obscurations will definitely end.
Even if certainty does not arise,
this is meeting the dharmakāya.

When the nondual, innate
realization perfectly arises,
all the bad karma that has been accumulated
throughout beginningless time will, without exception,
be instantaneously, totally vanquished,
like darkness by a lamp.

The ignorant make the error of analyzing
all-accomplishing mahāmudrā in terms of paths and levels.
So here, too, in order to please the ignorant,
I will give an analysis of its correspondence
with the paths and levels of the Vehicle of Characteristics
   (Lakṣanayāna).[95]

The perfect arising of realization
is the path of seeing, the level (*bhūmi*) of Perfect Joy.
Familiarization with the realization
of one taste is the path of meditation.
Nonmeditation is the path of complete accomplishment.

As soon as nonduality is realized,
even though suffering is not yet eliminated
and the power of the qualities are not developed,
who can say that this isn't the path of seeing?

When the sun rises in the morning,
it does not immediately melt the ice,
and the ground and stones stay cold,
but who can deny that it's the sun?

The stages of the paths and levels
and all the individual, particular signs of heat
are nonliteral teachings given by Śākyamuni
as provisional truths for pupils who pass through stages.

The ignorant are attached to temporary things,
and there are countless higher and lower grades of pupils,
and so the Buddha's teachings are countless too.
If there is a teaching that conflicts with your own tradition,
do not malign it or reject it
but pray that you'll eventually understand it.

The all-accomplishing mahāmudrā
has, like the jackfruit,
a simultaneous cause and result;[96]
it is conceptualization liberating itself.

Monkeys have to climb to get fruit,
but crows just fly down to get them.
It's evident that crows get to the fruit
without even having to see the branches.

In the same way it's evident
that immediate individuals attain the dharmakāya
without even seeing the signs of heat in the paths and levels.

Whatever their individual training and capabilities,
the instant they realize the natural state,
they attain the kingdom of nirvana.
From then on they know the result to be
this pure nature of the mind, which has no attainment.

This knowledge or realization is without conceptual identification;
it is natural liberation, without meditation or post-meditation,
    without birth or death.
This is liberation as Vajradhara,
which means the natural presence of the five kāyas.

It is taught that omniscience
is attained through completing the two accumulations
and purifying the two obscurations.
In this, too, the two accumulations are completed
and the two obscurations spontaneously purified.

When nonduality is realized,
this instantly pleases all gurus and buddhas,

which completes the great accumulation of merit,
and you are permanently purified
of the seeds of miserliness and other obscuring afflictions.

While you are becoming familiarized with this realization,
there remains the subtlest obscuration of knowledge,
but the instant there is nonmeditation,
the great accumulation of wisdom is completed,
and you are permanently purified of the seeds of the triple
    aspects [of conceptualization],
which is the obscuration of knowledge.

This is what is called complete enlightenment.
This is the accomplishment of mahāmudrā.

E ma! This wonderful, marvelous Dharma
brings complete buddhahood in an instant!

11. Impartiality

The true nature in that view,
and all other qualities, such as meditation,
conduct, commitment, and result,
are all manifestations of your own mind.

The mind is a state of clear self-knowing.
That clarity has an empty nature, like space;
it cannot be divided.
There are no directions, center, or periphery.

There is no duality of viewer and viewed
in the nature of the mind.
Therefore there is no view and no realization.

There is no duality of meditator and object of meditation.
Therefore there is no meditation and no experience.

There is no duality of familiarizer and familiarized.
Therefore there is no familiarization and no absence of
    familiarization.

There is no duality of someone distracted and an object of
    distraction.
Therefore there is no nondistraction and no distraction.

There is no duality of performer of conduct and performed
    conduct.
Therefore there is no conduct and nothing that is performed.

There is no duality of someone who attains and something
    attained.
Therefore there is no accomplishment and no attainment.

There is no duality of cause and result,
just like the center of empty space.
Therefore there is no generation and no ripening.

There is no obscuration and no purification
in the mind that is primordially empty;
it is the immaterial inseparability of knowing and emptiness.
Therefore there is no wisdom and no ignorance.

The meditators who thus know,
in the luminous essence of the mind,
the equality of view, meditation,
conduct, commitment, and result
have no attachment to a viewer and a viewed.
Therefore they are the kings of attachment-free view.

They have no attachment to a meditator and object of
   meditation.
Therefore they are the kings of attachment-free meditation.

They have no attachment to a performer of conduct and a performed conduct.
Therefore they are the kings of attachment-free conduct.

They have no attachment to someone who attains and something attained.
Therefore they are the kings of attachment-free result.

12. The White Panacea

In the instant that you realize your own mind,
all good qualities, without exception,
are simultaneously completed without having to accomplish
   them.

The three kāyas are primordially, naturally present
in the nature of the mind, which is like space;
the Jewel of the Buddha is complete within it.

The nature of the mind is free of elaboration, free of desire;
the Jewel of the Dharma is complete within it.

Its nature is birthless and irreversible,
with the variety of thoughts arising as its companions;
the Jewel of the Sangha is complete within it.

Even the Three Jewels
are complete in your own mind's knowing.
There is therefore no need to seek refuge elsewhere;
the definitive refuge is complete in it.

In the nature of the mind, which is without elaboration,
there is no basis for desire and selfishness.
Therefore the aspirational bodhicitta is complete in it.

Everything is understood to be an illusion,
so that objectless compassion arises
and benefiting others is naturally present.
Therefore the engaged bodhicitta is complete in that.

In the nature of the mind, which is like space,
there is freedom from all fixation and attachment.
Therefore the perfection of generosity is complete in that.

It is perfectly pure of the stains of concepts.
Therefore the perfection of conduct is complete in that.

There is no fear of emptiness, the seeds of anger are
    vanquished.
Therefore the perfection of patience is complete in that.

The union of knowing and emptiness is never interrupted.
Therefore the perfection of diligence is complete in that.

One-pointedness is primordially, naturally present.
Therefore the perfection of meditation is complete in that.

There is spontaneous liberation from the concepts of wrong
    views.
Therefore the perfection of wisdom is complete in that.

Everything that appears arises as companions.
Therefore the great method, the great accumulation of merit,
    is complete in that.

The meaning of nonduality is realized.
Therefore the great accumulation of wisdom is complete in that.

In the nature of the mind, which is like space,
there are no stains whatsoever from the body.
Therefore the supreme vase empowerment is complete in that.

There is primordial purity from the stains of speech.
Therefore the supreme secret empowerment is complete in that.

There is no location for the stains of the mind.
Therefore the supreme empowerment of the prajñā's wisdom[97]
    is complete in that.

There is no location for stains that come equally from body,
    speech, and mind.
Therefore the supreme fourth empowerment is complete in
    that.

The naturally clear knowing is unceasing
and appears as every kind of body, color, and insignia.
Therefore every kind of generation stage is complete in that.

The clarity has no conceptual identification.
Therefore the completion stage is complete in that.

The superior realization of your own mind as
nondual luminosity is the path of seeing,
its unbroken continuity is the path of meditation,
its effortlessness is the path of complete attainment.

Not being limited by anything is the supreme sign of heat.
Therefore the signs of heat on the paths and levels are com-
    plete in that.

Being nothing whatsoever: that is the dharmakāya.
Appearing as anything whatsoever: that is the nirmāṇakāya.
All that appears is enjoyed (*saṃbhoga*) as the dharmakāya.
Therefore the resultant three kāyas are complete in that.

As there is no partiality in self-knowing,
which is like space, the view is complete in that.
As there is no attachment to objects of perception, meditation
    is complete in that.
As there is no adoption or rejection, conduct is complete in
    that.
As there is no loss, commitment is complete in that.
As there is natural presence, the result is complete in that.

There are no three times, there is no before and after,
in the empty luminosity of the mind.

For as long as there is fixation upon a self,
there will be view, meditation, conduct, result, and
    commitment,
and there will be karma and the ripening of karma.
So it's essential to avoid bad actions and accumulate merit.

13. Prayer

I, the beggar monk from Shang,
on the urging of Chökyi Lodrö, my attendant,
have written these conceptual embellishments
for the purpose of guiding a few pupils
to the true nature of their own minds,
which is primordially devoid of conceptual embellishment.

It was not wrong to write this, for it was written with love
and with the thought that anything is possible.

May this good action and all other good actions,
without exception, become one
and cause the nondual dharmakāya to appear
to all beings throughout space.

May objectless compassion, free of attachment,
effortlessly spread form kāyas to the ends of space
in order to benefit beings,
manifesting whatever is necessary to train them.

From this day onward, throughout all time,
may I obtain a perfect existence of freedoms and
    opportunities
and, with faith, wisdom, and compassion,
apply myself solely to powerful, good conduct.

May I always be a perfect vessel for the supreme Vajrayāna,
have the instructions of the perfect guru,
gain the supreme realization with his compassionate blessing,
and always please him.

May I continuously see the guru's qualities,
never see a single fault,
and with uninterrupted faith and veneration
always see him as Vajradhara.

With great, objectless compassion
unstained by negative motivation,
may I attain all the qualities
of every guru and buddha.

May I attain the pure view, free from the bias
that leads to the marginal extremes of eternalism and nihilism.

May I attain bliss, clarity, and nonthought, free from
    attachment,
and may I attain the supreme conduct of one taste.

May I never shame the ḍākinīs but always apply myself
to keeping and practicing the commitments,
unblemished by the stains of afflictions,
deception, and pretense.

May I always wander in the mountains,
never experiencing fear, sadness, or obstacles.
May I attain powerful miracles and qualities,
such as experiences, realizations, and signs of heat.

May my gurus, Dharma companions,
and all other beings
see whatever conduct I perform
as pleasing.

May seeing, hearing, remembering, and touching
my body, speech, and mind,
my dwelling, clothes, name, family, and so on
fulfill whatever desires others have.

May I give away all things, without attachment.
May I not have faults such as hope and desire.
May I have a pure conduct, an undisturbed mind,
and realize an ever joyful, undistracted knowledge.

May I attain stability in the generation and completion
    practices;
may I gain the final goal of union and luminosity
and fulfill the hopes of the six classes of beings
with naturally present blessings.

The Mind of Mahāmudrā

May I, through objectless compassion,
powers, and miracles beyond measure,
tame all powerful, worldly deities
such as devas, nāgas, yakṣas, and māras.

When the time comes to benefit beings,
may I, without regret, happily and perfectly
give away my head, my legs, my arms,
my flesh, my blood, my breath, and everything else.

May I, without pride, provide the unending
benefit of whatever is needed,
every possession that is desired,
such as food, drink, jewels, and steeds.

May my glorious power give protection
from all dangers from enemies and demons,
from the dangers of suffering,
such as sickness and famine.

From this day on, throughout all time,
may I act only to benefit others.
May I, without being disturbed or saddened,
benefit others, no matter what wrongs they have done.

May I benefit all beings,
without arrogance, pride, or envy,
without self-interest, bias, or partiality,
and unblemished by the stain of bad actions.

May I not delight in such things as praise from others
and not be displeased by such things as criticism
but have the effortless compassion of equanimity,
unblemished by the stains of attachment and aversion.

May the compassion of Avalokiteśvara,
the wisdom of Mañjughoṣa,
and the power of Vajrapāṇi
be totally complete within me.

May I attain the entirety of
the knowledge of Nāgārjunagarbha,
the realization of Saraha,
and the power of Virūpa.

May I know the practices of every tantra,
accomplish all activity rites without impediment,
be the master of countless instructions,
and please all of the ḍākinīs.

May there be benefit for others through the eternal,
definitive realization of the meaning of equality:
no phenomenon comes from anywhere,
goes anywhere, or is present anywhere.

May I, for the sake of others, be free from the fault of desire,
become skilled, without bias,
in the arts, commentaries, poetry, and so on,
and never be defeated by opponents in debate.

May I never lack any favorable conditions,
such as family, qualities, possessions,
unmistaken words and meanings,
wisdom, power, and confidence.

14. Colophon

Nowadays, in these evil times, it is rare for Dharma
    practitioners

to tame their behavior and speech with study.
Though skilled in words, they don't realize their meaning,
which results in an increase in arrogance and quarreling.

We should follow and accomplish the meaning
taught by the venerable gurus of the practice lineage,
completely eliminating pride and so on,
and realize the meaning, which fulfills the purpose of scripture
and logic.

Tilopa did not speak
a single word to Nāropa,
yet all scripture, logic, and instruction
became complete in Nāropa's mind.

Therefore this chattering of mine,
though eloquent in its expression of humility and so on,
has the faults of contradiction, connection, calculation, and
repetition,
and it is comprised of empty, unexamined words.

Nevertheless there is the faintest possibility that
when passed on to my pupils it will help them.
That is why I've written this.
If a single word of it contradicts
scripture, logic, or the instructions, may my head split open!

This is the extent of beggar monk Shang's realization.
I wrote it on the urging of Marpa, my attendant,
in front of the Pangbuthul cliffs.

Do not show this to people or you will accumulate bad
karma.

This has been my description of the words of the Buddha, their commentaries, the viewpoints of the sublime gurus, and my own realization.

Ithiḥ[98]

3. A Record of Mahāmudrā Instructions

Drukchen Pema Karpo

Due to his literary output, Pema Karpo (1527–92) is the most well-known lama in the Drukpa Kagyü tradition and one of the great authors of Tibetan Buddhism. The Drukpa Kagyü lineage has its origin with Lingré Pema Dorjé (1128–88), who started out as a Rechung Kagyüpa. Rechungpa's lineage was not monastic, its practice involving a tantric consort. However, in 1165 he became a pupil of Phakmo Drupa, one of the principal pupils of Gampopa, the founder of the monastic form of the Kagyü. On Phakmo Drupa's instruction, Lingré Pema Dorjé separated from his consort and subsequently practiced peripatetically around Central Tibet. He performed rites to ensure victory for Lama Shang in his battles, and in his last years he was the abbot of Naphur Monastery.

His pupil Tsangpa Gyaré (1161–1211)[99] founded Namdruk Monastery, from which the Drukpa lineage derives its name. The hereditary lineage of Tsangpa Gyaré's monastery became the principal succession in the Drukpa Kagyü. After Kunga Paljor (1428–76) declared himself the rebirth of Tsangpa Gyaré and became known as the Second Drukchen, there were both hereditary and incarnation successions.

Pema Karpo was the Fourth Drukchen, but after his passing the Drukpa Kagyü split into two, with two factions recognizing a different boy as the Drukchen. One of these was Ngawang Namgyal (1594–1651), who was also the hereditary successor. However, the king of Tsang, the greatest secular power in Tibet before the rise of the Fifth Dalai Lama, supported his rival Paksam Wangpo (1593–1653), who became the Fifth Drukchen. As a result Ngawang Namgyal and his followers created the independent state of Bhutan, where the succession of incarnations are known as Shapdrung.[100]

This short text on mahāmudrā practice by Pema Karpo presents thirty-one stages of meditation. It is widely used for instruction both within and outside the Drukpa Kagyü lineage because of its brevity, clarity, and practicality.

I PAY HOMAGE to the precious Kargyü.[101]

These are the instructions for the mahāmudrā innate union, which is a direct introduction to the continuum of the ordinary mind as true wisdom. It is in three parts: preliminaries, main part, and conclusion.

Preliminaries

These are of two kinds, general and special. The general preliminaries are clearly explained elsewhere.

The special preliminaries

First one does the practices of taking refuge and so on, up to guru yoga. Then, as taught in the *Enlightenment of Vairocana*:[102]

> Straighten the body, perform the vajra posture.
> The mind is one-pointed mahāmudrā.

Thus there are these seven Dharmas of Vairocana: (1) Sit with the legs in vajra posture. (2) Arrange the hands in the meditation mudrā below the navel. (3) Straighten the spine. (4) Broaden the shoulders. (5) Bend the throat like a hook, with the chin just pressing on the Adam's apple. (6) Place the tongue against the upper palate. (7) In general, your mind is changed by your senses, and in particular by the eyes. Therefore gaze a yoke's distance in front of you, without closing or moving the eyes.

There is also the presentation, in terms of function, of the five Dharmas of dhyāna: (1) The crossed legs cause the downward-expelling wind to enter the central channel. (2) The meditation mudrā causes the fire-like wind to enter the central channel. (3) The straightened spine and straightened abdomen cause the pervading wind to enter the central channel. (4) The bent throat causes the upward-moving wind to enter the central channel. (5) The tongue against the upper palate and the gaze cause the *prāṇa* (the life-force wind) to enter the central channel.

As a result of those five winds entering the central channel, every karmic wind enters the central channel, and nonconceptual wisdom arises. This is called the *solitude of the body*, the *unmoving body*, and the *naturally resting body*.

Expelling the stale breath and remaining silent is called the *solitude of the speech*, the *unmoving speech*, and the *naturally resting speech*.

Do not contemplate the past. Do not think of the future. Do not meditate by deliberate application of the intellect. Do not view "emptiness" as nonexistence. Do not examine or analyze whatever appears in the present as the objects of the five senses using thoughts such as "is" or "isn't" but look inward. Be loose, like a baby, letting the mind rest naturally, without an instant's distraction.

> Cast away all thinking and thoughts
> and be like a relaxed, resting baby.
> If one keeps to the guru's transmission and makes a
>   devoted effort,
> there is no doubt but that the innate will appear.[103]

According to Tilopa:

> Do not contemplate, do not think, do not analyze,
> do not meditate, do not mentate, but rest naturally.[104]

According to the Dharma king Kumāra Candraprabha:[105]

> Nondistraction is the path of all buddhas.[106]

This is called the *solitude of the mind*, the *unmoving mind*, and the *naturally resting mind*.

According to Nāgārjuna:

> Lord, mindfulness within the body is taught to be
> the one path that has been traversed by the sugatas.
> Discipline yourself in that and truly protect it.
> If mindfulness is lost, then all Dharma is destroyed.[107]

That is mindfulness without distraction. From the Abhidharma:

> Mindfulness is not forgetting the object with which
> one has become familiar.[108]

Main practice

This is in two parts, general practices and special practices.

General practices

This is in two parts: (1) seeking the experience of the basis of meditation: the meditation of one-pointed yoga, and (2) analyzing the basis of stillness and movement and identifying it through vipaśyanā: the meditation of elaboration-free yoga.

Seeking the experience of the foundation of meditation: the meditation of one-pointed yoga

This is in two parts, meditation with a base and meditation without a base.

One-pointed yoga meditation with a base

This is in two parts: (1) meditation without the breath as a base and (2) meditation with the breath as a base.

Without the breath as a base

This is in two parts: (1) arranging an object such as a pebble or little stick as an impure base and (2) arranging a representation of the Tathāgata's body, speech, or mind as a pure base.

Meditation upon an object such as a pebble or little stick as an impure base

MEDITATION 1

Place in front of you a little pebble as the base for your focus. Do not allow your mind to wander externally or be absorbed internally but look one-pointedly on that object alone.

Meditate that the guru is on the crown of your head and think that he is truly a buddha. Recite the "My mothers throughout space" prayer.[109] Request his blessing by reciting, "I pray that you give your blessing for the attainment of the supreme siddhi of mahāmudrā," and think that the guru merges into you so that your minds are blended. Rest in meditation for as long as you are able. Meditate that every state of mind that suddenly appears blends with the guru.

If the mind becomes dulled, raise your gaze and meditate in a place that has a wide-open space. If the mind sinks into a stupor, clarify it with mindfulness as just described. If the mind is agitated, sit in a solitary place, gaze downward, and most of all relax.

Meditation upon the Tathāgata's body, speech, and mind as a pure base

This is in three parts: (1) an image of the Buddha's body as a base, (2) a letter of the Buddha's speech as a base, and (3) a quintessence (*bindu*) of the Buddha's mind as a base.

Meditation upon an image of the Buddha's body as a pure base

MEDITATION 2

Focus the mind continuously upon the Buddha, either a statue, a painting, or a visualization that resembles a golden statue: yellow, adorned by the primary and secondary signs, radiating light, and wearing the three Dharma robes.

Meditation upon a syllable of the Buddha's speech as a pure base

MEDITATION 3

Meditate that in front of you, upon a moon disc the size of a pea, stands a *hūṃ* that is written as if with a single hair.

Meditation upon a quintessence of the Buddha's mind as a pure base

MEDITATION 4

Focus the mind as previously described upon the special symbol of an egg-shaped spheroid that is the size of a pea and shines with light.

With breath as the base

This is in two parts: based upon vajra repetition and based upon vase breathing.

Meditation upon the breath based upon vajra repetition

MEDITATION 5

Allow the mind and body to rest naturally and focus the mind upon the inhalation and exhalation of the breath. Count the breaths from one, two, and so on, until 21,600. As a result, you will become knowledgeable in the number of the inner and outer movements of the breath.

MEDITATION 6

During the exhalation and inhalation, think that the breath moves throughout the body, or through just one part of it, and follow the exhalation and inhalation of the breath in that way. As a result, you will become knowledgeable in the characteristics of the breath.

MEDITATION 7

Blend your consciousness with the breath and observe it moving from the tip of the nose down to the navel, resting, and coming back up. As a result, you will see the color and length of the individual winds.

MEDITATION 8

Examine the five elements individually, without mixing them. As a result, you will know the waxing and waning of the inner and outer movements of the breath.

MEDITATION 9

The exhalation becomes a white *oṃ* syllable, the inhalation a blue *hūṃ*, and the resting a red *āḥ*. As a result, there will be the cessation of the outer and inner movements of breath.

Meditation upon the breath based upon the vase breathing

MEDITATION 10

Expel the stale breath three times. Slowly inhale the upper air through the nose. Draw up the lower air and apply yourself to holding it as much as you can. That which is called the *mind difficult to completely tame* is focused upon as being nothing other than wind, so that when the movement of wind ceases, thoughts that stray toward objects will also cease.

One-pointed yoga meditation without a base

This is in three parts: (1) the complete cutting through of suddenly appearing thoughts, (2) not changing whatever arises, and (3) the key point for resting the mind.

The complete cutting through of suddenly appearing thoughts

MEDITATION 11

If, while meditating as described above on the arising of a thought, the mind becomes involved with an object of thought, clarify the mind with mindfulness, thinking, "I must not have even a single thought that will cause me to continue with this thinking." Meditate on repeatedly cutting through the arising of suddenly appearing thoughts.

MEDITATION 12

When you extend the above meditation, thoughts will eventually multiply until in the end one thought will come on top of another in an unbroken continuity. Identifying these thoughts is like recognizing an enemy. It is the first stage [of śamatha], which is like a river rushing down a steep mountainside. The mind is aware of the arising and ceasing of thoughts because it is at rest in every instant. The result is that it seems as if thoughts are multiplying, but thoughts have always been rising, so there is no change in their quantity. It's the nature of thoughts to arise one moment and cease the next.

Not changing whatever arises

MEDITATION 13

Meditate by allowing thoughts to go wherever they wish, while having your own mind spy on them without stopping them or falling under their power. This will result in a one-pointed śamatha that cannot be disrupted by thoughts.

MEDITATION 14

Thoughts and so on continue to move rapidly, but by meditating as before, states of stability will last longer. This is the middle stage of stability, which is like a slowly flowing river. This key point of naturally resting the mind will make it become clear.

According to the Dharma lord [Gampopa]:

> If the mind is unaltered, it becomes happy.
> If water is not disturbed, it becomes clear.[110]

According to the great lord of yoga [Lingrepa]:[111]

> If you rest in unaltered freshness, there will be realization.
> If you can maintain this like the flow of a river, realization will be complete.
> Oh yogins! Completely abandon all ideas of focusing the mind
> and rest continuously in equanimity.[112]

Concerning these two kinds of meditation, Saraha has taught the following:

If it is bound, it will attempt to flee into the ten
    directions.
If it is set free, it will not move and be still.
I have understood this paradox, which is just like a
    camel.[113]

The key point for resting the mind

This is in four parts: (1) resting like weaving a brahman's thread,
(2) resting like a sheaf of hay after its cord has been cut, (3) resting like a baby looking at a temple, and (4) resting like an elephant being pricked by a thorn.

Resting like weaving a brahman's thread

MEDITATION 15

A thread should be woven so that it is neither too tight nor too loose. In the same way, if your meditation is too tight, you lose it in thoughts; if it's too loose, you will lose it in idleness. Therefore you must have the right balance between being too tight or too loose. Beginners should be tighter at first, cutting through the sudden arising of thoughts. Then when that becomes tiring, they should become looser by not altering whatever thoughts arise. By alternating these two approaches, a natural balance between being too tight and too loose will develop. Therefore it's taught that mind should first be tightened and then loosened and relaxed, as when weaving a brahman's thread.

Resting like a sheaf of hay after its cord has been cut

MEDITATION 16

Think that all previous remedies were just the arising of thoughts and that all you need is to be undistracted. Stopping thoughts is merely a remedy, and "mindfulness in pursuit" stains meditation, so abandon that kind of mindfulness and awareness and rest naturally in the continuum of śamatha. This resting, free from any mental effort, is like a sheaf of hay after its cord has been cut.

Resting like a baby looking at a temple

MEDITATION 17

When you tie the elephant of the mind firmly to the post of mindfulness and awareness, the breath will become naturally stilled. This will result in seeing empty forms, such as smoke and so on; you will almost faint with bliss; there will be a state of nonthought that is like empty space with no physical or mental sensations and so on. However, whatever kind of experiences you have, neither be pleased with them nor see them as faults. Don't fixate on them or stop them from occurring. Neither stopping nor fixating on appearances, which never cease, is like a baby looking at a temple.

Resting like an elephant being pricked by a thorn

MEDITATION 18

When a thought arises in a state of stability, simultaneously there is mindfulness that is aware of it. As the remedy and the fault are in direct contact, the thought cannot lead to a second thought. There is no deliberate application of a remedy; instead there is the "spontaneous maintenance of mindfulness." You experience thoughts arising while simply remaining at rest, without either stopping or creating them. This is the meaning of resting "like an elephant being pricked by a thorn."[114]

That is the last stage of stability, which is said to be like an ocean without waves. In this state of stability, there is the self-recognition of the mind's movements, and while there are these movements, the stability continues. Therefore this is called *eliminating the distinction between stability and movement.* That is the self-recognition in the one-pointed state.

That which recognizes this stability and movement is called *correct attention* or *discriminating wisdom* or *self-knowing.* From *Ornament of the Mahayana Sutras*:

> Therefore through that, one attains
> great functionality of mind and body
> as well as attention and analytic knowledge.[115]

Analyzing the basis of stillness and movement and identifying it through vipaśyanā: the meditation of yoga without elaboration

This is in three parts: (1) analysis of the root of stillness and movement, (2) recognition through vipaśyanā, (3) yoga without elaboration.

Analysis of the root of stillness and movement

MEDITATION 19

When nonconceptual śamatha has become discriminating wisdom, it analyzes stillness to see what its essence is, how it is still, how movement comes from it, whether stability is lost or persists when there is movement, what the nature of movement is, and how it ceases.

MEDITATION 20

There is no movement separate from the stability and there is no stability that is separate from movement; so you won't find that stability or movement has an essence.

In that case, is that viewer's knowing different from the stability or movement that it is looking at, or is it itself the stability and the movement?

The analysis with the eyes of self-knowing does not result in finding anything, so that you realize the inseparability of the viewer and the viewed. No essence whatsoever can be located. Therefore this is called the *view that transcends the intellect* and the *view without an assertion*. According to the lord of conquerors:

> The mentally fabricated view is excellent but destructible.
> That which transcends the intellect does not even have
>   the name "view."
> It is through the guru's kindness that you attain
> certainty in the inseparability of the viewer and the
>   viewed.[116]

Ācārya Śāntideva has taught this kind of analysis:

> Be dedicated to concentration
> without losing it for an instant;
> examine your own mind
> to see what it is doing.[117]

There is the example of fire and firewood from the *Sutra Requested by Kāśyapa*:

> Fire comes from two sticks being rubbed together;
> its appearance burns up the two sticks.
> In the same way, when the power of wisdom appears,
> its appearance burns up both those two.[118]

This kind of analysis is the analysis of the inward-looking, self-knowing. It is called *kusali's analytic meditation*. It isn't the paṇḍita's analytic meditation, because that is an outward-looking knowledge.

Recognition through vipaśyanā

MEDITATION 21

Whatever thoughts or afflictions arise, don't reject them. Without falling under their power, let all things that arise be just what they are, without altering them. Recognize them at the very instant they arise so that, without eliminating them, their arising is naturally purified as emptiness. In this way, you can transform all adverse factors into the path. This is called *bringing conditions into the path*.

Thoughts are liberated simply by recognizing them, which means you have realized the inseparability of the remedy and the remedied. This realization is the essence of the practice of the Vajrayāna and is called *paradoxical meditation*.

Exceptional compassion will arise for all beings who have not realized the nature of their own minds. This transcends methods of body, speech, and mind that are practiced for the sake of all beings, such as the generation stage. This wisdom purifies you of all attachment to reality such that there will be no afflictions. It's like consuming poison that has been blessed by mantras. It's taught that with this view of practice, whatever path you follow will be "without adoption or rejection."

Yoga without elaboration

This is in three parts: (1) analysis of past, present, and future, (2) analysis of things and nothing, and (3) analysis of singleness and multiplicity.

Analysis of past, present, and future

MEDITATION 22

The past mind has ceased, is destroyed; the future mind is not born, has not arisen; the present mind cannot be identified.

When you analyze in that way, you will see that all phenomena are like that. Nothing has reality; everything is just a creation of the mind. Therefore you will understand that arising, remaining, and ceasing have no reality at all. Analyze as taught by Saraha:

> The arising of things has a nature like space,
> so when things are eliminated, what can arise afterward?
> Their nature is primordial birthlessness.
> Realize today what the lord guru has taught![119]

Analysis of things and nothing

MEDITATION 23

Examine in this way: Does your mind exist? Is it a real thing? Or does it not exist? Is it nothing? If it exists as a thing, is it the perceiver or the perceived? If it is perceived, what is its shape and color? If it is the perceiver, there would be nothing else. If it is nothing, then what creates all this variety of appearances? Examine in this way.

If there is an existent essence, then that essence can be established, but your cognition's examination does not find anything that exists. There is nothing to be found that can be established as existent, as having the quality of a thing. As this is the province of self-knowing, it is not nonexistence or nothingness.

Therefore, as there is neither a thing nor nothing, you do not fall into the paths of eternalism or nihilism. Therefore this is called the *middle-way path*. This does not come from establishing reasons or gaining certainty through negations. It is through the guru's instructions that you see it clearly, like a jewel in the palm of your hand. That is why it's called the *great middle way*.

> When the guru's words enter your heart,
> it's like seeing a treasure in the palm of your hand.[120]

Analysis of singleness and multiplicity

MEDITATION 24

Is this mind single or multiple? If you say it's single, this word *mind* is used for something that has various manifestations, so how can it be single? If you say it's a multiplicity, how could they all be the same in the mind's empty essence? Thus, the mind transcends multiple or not multiple. This is called the *completely unlocated mahāmudrā*.

In the meditation of the practitioners who have this realization, there is only their own self-knowing, and there is nothing else that appears. Therefore it is called *devoid of appearances*.

In the post-meditation period, everything appears as an illusion, because this path has purified them of attachment to anything as being real. Thus [according to Saraha]:

> Lord, someone like me has today cut through delusion!
> So it doesn't matter what I see,
> in front, behind, or in the ten directions;
> I no longer have a question for anyone![121]

Special practices

This is in two parts: (1) the yoga of one taste: the equal taste of all phenomena as the inseparability of mind and appearances, and (2) the yoga of nonmeditation: the certainty that all phenomena are the natural, innate dharmakāya.

The yoga of one taste: the equal taste of all phenomena as the inseparability of mind and appearances

This is in three parts: (1) recognizing appearances as mind through the example of a dream, (2) recognizing the unity of appearances and emptiness through the example of water and ice, and (3) gaining certainty in the equal taste of all phenomena through the example of water and waves.

Recognizing appearances as mind through the example of a dream

MEDITATION 25

During sleep, whatever appears is nothing other than the mind. In the same way, all present appearances are also the dreams of ignorant sleep and are nothing other than your own mind. If you rest, relaxed, on whatever apparent objects appear, the externally appearing object and what is called "one's own mind" become blended indivisibly into one taste. According to the lord of yoga:

> The experiences of last night's dreams
> are teachers that show you that appearances
> are the mind. Do you understand that?[122]

And also [according to Saraha]:

> Transform the colors of the entirety of these three
> realms into the single great desire.[123]

Recognizing the unity of appearances and emptiness through the example of water and ice

MEDITATION 26

All phenomena that appear, at the very time that they appear, have no existent essence. Therefore they are called "empty." In the same way, though they have no existence whatsoever, they appear as anything whatsoever. Therefore they are said to be the *union of appearance and emptiness*, or the *one taste*, as in the example of ice and water. Knowing in the same way the union of emptiness and bliss, emptiness and clarity, and emptiness and knowing is called the *realization of the one taste of the many*.

> When that is realized, everything is that.
> No one can know anything that is other than that.
> That is what is read, memorized, and meditated on.[124]

Gaining certainty in the equal taste of all phenomena through the example of water and waves

MEDITATION 27

Waves arise from water. In the same way, all phenomena are created by the nature of your mind, which is emptiness, arising as every kind of appearance. Saraha has taught that:

> Whatever is manifested from the mind
> has at that time the nature of the Lord.[125]

The single true nature pervades the entire expanse of phenomena. This is called the *one taste arising as many*. For the practitioners who realize this, their subsequent knowledge will arise as all-pervading emptiness.

The yoga of nonmeditation: the certainty that all phenomena are the natural, innate dharmakāya

MEDITATION 28

As the afflictions that were to be eliminated have ceased, the eliminating remedies also cease and the path ends. There is nowhere else to go. There is nothing more to enter. You cannot get any higher. You have attained the unlocated nirvana, the supreme siddhi of mahāmudrā. From the "blending" teaching [of Tilopa]:

Kyeho! This is self-knowing wisdom!
It transcends the path of speech; it cannot be experienced by the mind.
I, Tilopa,[126] have nothing to teach.
Know that it is revealed to you by yourself.[127]

It is also the meaning of this teaching [by Tilopa]:

Do not contemplate, do not think, do not analyze,
do not meditate, do not mentate, but rest naturally.[128]

The conclusion

This is in three parts: (1) the recognition: direct introduction to the mahāmudrā, (2) analysis of obstacles and errors, and (3) distinguishing comprehension, experience, and realization.

The recognition: direct introduction to the mahāmudrā

MEDITATION 29

The four yogas that manifest the result are:
 1. Gaining certainty in the basis
 2. Practicing the path
 3. Distinguishing the details of experiences
 4. Distinguishing the signs of heat on the paths and the stages

Analysis of obstacles and errors

MEDITATION 30

Knowing that appearances are mind eliminates the obstacle of appearances arising as enemies. Knowing that thoughts are the dharmakāya eliminates [the obstacle of] thoughts arising as enemies. Knowing the union of appearance and emptiness eliminates [the obstacle of] emptiness arising as an enemy.

The *three errors*[129] are attachments to the experience of śamatha. Enhancing vipaśyanā eliminates them. The *four mistakes* are mistakes concerning the nature of emptiness. Emptiness arising as compassion eliminates them.

The correct realization of the way things are eradicates mistakes in "sealing." The inseparability of the "remedy and the remedied" eradicates mistakes in remedy. The realization of the simultaneity of arising and liberation brings to an end the mistakes of the path.

Distinguishing comprehension, experience, and realization

MEDITATION 31

Comprehension is the realization gained through hearing about and contemplating the nature of the mind. *Experience* is one-pointed, general realization. *Realization* is direct realization, from the level of "freedom from conceptual elaboration" upward. As the same word is used for them all, there is nothing wrong in calling them all *realization*.

* * *

Shenphen Sangpo, the king of Zangskar in Kashmir,[130] offered me over one load of saffron blossoms and asked me to write a record of instructions for both the mahāmudrā and the six Dharmas. As I have never found anything reliable among the many manuscript records of the oral tradition, I, Pema Karpo, while staying in the Bodhgaya of the southern land of Kharchu,[131] compiled this text solely in order to benefit future times.

May goodness result from this!

4. Instructions for the Mahāmudrā Innate Union

⎯⎯⎯⎯⎯⎯⎯⎯⎯⎯ ⚬⚬⚬ ⎯⎯⎯⎯⎯⎯⎯⎯⎯⎯

Karmapa Rangjung Dorjé

Düsum Khyenpa (1110–93), the future First Karmapa, was already an accomplished practitioner and a monk when he met Gampopa and Gomtsül in 1139.[132] He also subsequently received instructions from Rechungpa and practiced meditation with exceptional perseverance and disregard for personal comfort for many years in various locations.

In 1159, six years after Gampopa's death, he returned to his homeland in eastern Tibet, where he established Karma Monastery. In 1189, at the age of seventy-nine, he returned to Central Tibet and founded Tsurphu Monastery. He said that he had returned to fulfill a request by Gomtsül, who had died twenty years earlier, and to persuade the sixty-seven-year-old Lama Shang to terminate his martial exploits. Both Düsum Khyenpa and Lama Shang died four years later.

As the first in a succession of Karmapa rebirths, Düsum Khyenpa marks the beginning of the now ubiquitous *tulku* system of incarnate lamas. Gampopa, Lama Shang, and Düsum Khyenpa all recognized lamas and children as rebirths of great masters, but the Second Karmapa, Karma Pakshi (1204–83), was the first to inherit the monasteries and authority of his predecessor.[133]

The Third Karmapa, Rangjung Dorjé (1284–1339), author of the next two works translated here, established a Karma Kagyü canon of practice and study, introducing a number of teachings from other lineages. His prominence was such that he performed the enthronement ceremony for the thirteen-year-old emperor Togan Temur (r. 1333–70), the last Mongol to rule China before the rise of the Ming dynasty. Karmapa Rangjung Dorjé's writings form a large body of important texts. The first, less well-known text here is *Instructions for the Mahāmudrā Innate Union*. A practical manual for meditating on mahāmudrā, it guides the practitioner through successive stages of *śamatha* (stability) and *vipaśyanā* (insight) meditation. It was composed in 1324, when he was forty years old.

I PAY HOMAGE to the sublime gurus.

The truly perfect Buddha Vajradhara taught glorious great Tilopa[134] the introduction to the innate self-knowing wisdom. [Tilopa taught this] to glorious Nāropa after his twelve great hardships. This introduction to the meaning of realization given to the followers of this path is in three parts:
  1. The preliminaries
  2. The main practice, which consists of attaining a mental state of śamatha and an introduction to the innate meaning of vipaśyanā
  3. The conclusion

The preliminaries

THE FIRST MEDITATION

A true guru with the necessary qualities only gives this teaching to pupils who practice properly, have abandoned the activities of this life, and are intent on attaining unsurpassable enlightenment. First of all the guru gives the pupils the vows of correct conduct (śīla) and bodhicitta. Then the guru gives them empowerments that completely ripen them. Then they should practice in a pleasant and solitary place.

First, cutting through the body, speech, and mind's bondage to the world, sit in the key physical posture upon a comfortable seat: the legs are crossed, the hands are resting level, the waist is straight, the throat is bent, and the eyes are looking toward the tip of the nose. Sitting naturally in this way is the key point for the body.

Then meditate on compassion, sincerely thinking, "Oh, I

feel such pity for these beings who have been wandering in the ocean of samsara, experiencing countless sufferings throughout beginningless time. They are wandering in endless samsara because they have not realized their own minds to be the essence of buddhahood and have developed attachment to an I and a self."

Then develop devotion, thinking, "The sublime refuges are the kind buddhas. This guru who gives the teachings directly to me is performing the activity of a buddha for me and therefore is showing me even greater kindness than they do."

Meditate that Vajradhara, Vajrasattva, or your root guru is upon the crown of your head. He is an appearance without a real nature and is inseparable from all the buddhas and bodhisattvas in the ten directions and inseparable from all the Kagyü gurus. Offer your body and possessions to him, reciting:

> I pay homage to the glorious, sublime guru
> in the palace of Akaniṣṭha Dharmadhātu;
> he is the essence of all the buddhas in the three times
> and is the one who truly shows my own mind to be the
>   dharmakāya.
>
> I praise you and offer to you my body, my possessions,
> and all the offerings manifested by my mind.
> I confess to you every bad action I have done in the past,
> and from now on I will not do any other bad actions.
>
> I rejoice in the good actions of all beings.
> I make a dedication as a cause for supreme
>   enlightenment.
> I pray that you remain and do not pass into nirvana.
> I request that you turn the wheel of the unsurpassable
>   supreme vehicle.

Give me your blessing so that I will develop unbiased
    love and compassion
and will directly realize the ultimate, innate wisdom,
just as all the buddhas and bodhisattvas have realized it.

Give me your blessing so that I will realize my illusory
    body to be the nirmāṇakāya.
Give me your blessing so that I will realize my life-force
    to be the saṃbhogakāya.
Give me your blessing so that I will realize my own mind
    to be the dharmakāya.
Give me your blessing so that the three kāyas will mani-
    fest indivisibly.

Then one-pointedly rest in the meditation of the guru yoga.
If that becomes unclear or thoughts arise, meditate that the
guru yoga melts into light and just relax in the unaltered mind.
At the conclusion of the sessions make a dedication, reciting:

May this be for the benefit of all beings.

In that way, just the essential posture of the body and the guru
yoga can develop samādhi. The Vinaya tells the story of how a
monkey who had watched a pratyekabuddha in this key physical posture taught it to five hundred non-Buddhist rishis, who
then attained the five kinds of clairvoyance, while the monkey
himself attained enlightenment.

Throughout the sutras and tantras appear scriptural passages
telling of how devotion to the guru and the buddhas is the cause
of enlightenment; so even though I will not relate them here,
believe it.

The main practice

This is in two parts, śamatha and vipaśyanā.

The causes of śamatha: the branch of dhyāna that is the meditation of focusing the mind

THE SECOND MEDITATION

The key physical posture is as before.

The gaze of the eyes should be directed at a point four finger-widths beyond the tip of the nose.

Do not follow the past, do not go forward to meet the future, but rest in present realization, in a state of clarity and nonthought.

If you cannot rest in the one-pointed inseparability of clarity and nonthought, meditate by relying on the six objects:

1. Direct your gaze upon any clear visual object and focus the mind upon it. Sometimes gaze upon something like a statue, sometimes on something like a twig or pebble. Keep your cognition focused on it, without interruption by any other thought.
2. When [meditation on a visual object] has become stable, meditate upon sound, such as the sound of water, the sound of the wind, the sounds of creatures, and so on, directing the mind to any clear sound and keeping it there.
3. When [meditation on sound] has become stable, focus the mind on whatever good or bad smell is experienced by the nose and meditate upon that.
4. Similarly, meditate by focusing the mind upon the delicious or unpleasant tastes that are experienced by the tongue.
5. In the same way, focus the mind on any distinct pleasant or unpleasant physical sensation.
6. When you are able to focus to some degree upon those [objects of meditation], meditate upon the phenomena

experienced by the mind, by the sixth consciousness. These consist of:

a. Composite mental phenomena
b. Noncomposite mental phenomena

Composite mental phenomena

THE THIRD MEDITATION

First, samsaric phenomena—thoughts that should be eliminated—such as desire, anger, pride, the five kinds of wrong views, and distraction-inducing thoughts caused by the primary and secondary afflictions: focus your awareness one-pointedly upon whichever of these appears clearly as an object of thought and meditate. Focus also on remedial thoughts, upon whatever arises in a virtuous mind, keeping the mind one-pointedly on them without interruption from any other thought. If you know this key point of mindfully focusing the mind, then whatever thought appears, there will be stability unaffected by dullness or agitation.

However, some people think they must forcefully stop thoughts, which are things to be eliminated. This is an extra obstacle on top of the instability of their minds and makes it difficult to develop samādhi. In relation to this, from *Ornament of the Mahayana Sutras*:

> Because of engaging correctly
> with that desire and so on,
> there will definitely be liberation from them.
> Therefore those liberations definitely arise from them.[135]

From the *Hevajra Tantra*:

> Through desire, beings become bound;
> through desire itself, they become liberated.[136]

That is what is meant by being skillful in method. *Distinguishing the Middle Way from the Extremes* also says:

> Objectlessness perfectly arises
> through dependence on an object.
> Objectlessness perfectly arises
> through dependence on objectlessness.
> Therefore an object is proved to be
> the very essence of objectlessness.
> As that is so, know that an object
> is the same as objectlessness.[137]

Therefore first focus the mind by concentrating on an object such as a visual form. Through a single concentration of the six consciousnesses, the mind's focusing on anything else will cease completely.

Noncomposite mental phenomena

THE FOURTH MEDITATION

When that meditation is stable, meditate on the noncomposite. Do not even use the six objects as bases for focusing the mind but leave the mind just as it is, without creating any thoughts whatsoever, without any concepts concerning appearances and emptiness, defects and remedies. Gaze into space with both eyes, with the body motionless, without speaking, and with a gentle and natural coming and going of the breath. Tilopa has said:

> Hold the mind as if it is space.[138]

Saraha has said:

> Make it like space and bind the breath evenly.

When there is complete knowledge of equality, it dissolves completely.
Saraha says that when you have this ability,
impermanent wavering will quickly be eliminated.[139]

This is what is to be understood when the *Perfection of Wisdom*
also says:

To make the perfection of wisdom your practice is to
make space your practice.[140]

If you meditate in that way, you will have good stability and will
establish an excellent cause for the development of dhyāna and
śamatha. In order to understand these aspects in detail, read my
teachings on the nine methods of mental stability and the eleven
mental engagements.[141] Śamatha's cause is reliance on correct
conduct; its essence is to be devoid of afflictions and thoughts;
its condition is the creation of an exceptional mental stability;
its benefit is the subjugation of coarse afflictions and sufferings.

The above was the stage of stabilizing the unstable mind.

The direct introduction that gives rise to vipaśyanā

THE FIFTH MEDITATION

Glorious Tilopa has said:

Kyeho! This is self-knowing wisdom!
It transcends the path of speech; it cannot be experi-
enced by the mind.
I, Tilopa, have nothing to teach.
Know that it is revealed to you by yourself.[142]

This means that having now stabilized the mind, you examine the manifestations of six consciousnesses within that state

of clarity and nonthought. Do the thoughts created by form, sound, smell, taste, physical sensation, and mental phenomena appear as external objects [of perception], or do they come from the eyes, the ears, the nose, the tongue, or the body? When you examine like this, you will see that the thoughts do not come from any of these. You will gain the certainty that the six objects and the five senses are naturally clear but nonconceptual.

The consciousnesses of the five senses—the visual consciousness that perceives forms, the auditory consciousness that perceives sounds, the olfactory consciousness that perceives smells, the gustatory consciousness that perceives tastes, and the tactile consciousness that perceives physical sensations—appear instantaneously in dependence on the sensory faculties and objects, and they are naturally clear and nonconceptual. Therefore, from among the six consciousnesses, that of the mind alone needs to be thoroughly examined.

When the mind is directed toward phenomena, such as the consciousnesses of the five senses, it is naturally clear and nonconceptual in every instant. Therefore there is no delusion within the six consciousnesses themselves.

When the previous consciousness has ceased and the subsequent consciousness has yet to appear, that which is in the present instant appears clearly. Therefore this relative truth is not to be rejected.

Although [the present consciousness] is clear, it does not exist as a shape and it does not exist as a color. Creators such as self, fate, Shiva, Brahma, atoms, unperceivable externals, puruṣa, and so on[143] have not created it. It is devoid of a real nature, and therefore the ultimate truth is not rejected.

Even appearances and emptiness are inseparable; they can appear as anything, can be called anything, and therefore are completely liberated from being itself or other. This is what you should realize.

"This is self-knowing" means that the unmistaken realization of that which is self-knowing is wisdom, because it knows the primordial true nature. Ordinary beings, who are like children, don't know how to describe that direct perception. It is not within the experience of the afflicted mind's thoughts. Therefore there is nothing to teach you until you have experienced it for yourself. This is also said in a doha:

> Don't disturb water or a lamp's flame; they are naturally
>   clear.
> I neither perform going and coming nor reject them.[144]

And also:

> *Kyeho!* This is self-knowing.
> Other than that there is nothing that can be directly
>   taught.
> Do not be deluded about this.[145]

Also, in *Summary of the View*:

> That elaboration-free self-knowing
> appears while empty and is empty while appearing.
> Therefore it is the inseparability of appearance and
>   emptiness.
> It is like the example of the moon on water.
> In this way gain certainty in nonduality.[146]

All texts have such teachings that can bring certainty through quotation and reasoning, but I shall stop here, so as to keep it simple. That concludes the introduction to the six consciousnesses.

Thus śamatha and vipaśyanā arise by resting in the clear and nonconceptual mind and becoming familiarized to the nature of self-knowing, to the inseparability of appearance and emptiness. The coarser afflictions will then be overcome, and you will enter the true path. Therefore the great masters of the past gave direct introductions by saying, "See the mind!" This stage accords with the following teaching:

> A vipaśyanā that has excellent śamatha
> is a knowledge that completely defeats the afflictions.
> Therefore first seek śamatha
> and accomplish it with true joy free from worldly
>   attachment.[147]

Next I will explain:

1. How the guru introduces you to your own nature and you have experiences
2. How you train with experiences
3. How you maximize the results

How the guru introduces you to your own nature and you have experiences

THE SIXTH MEDITATION

First, know the signs that indicate when meditation experiences are accompanied by realization or not. When the mind is controlled, dhyāna develops, from which come three benefits: bliss, clarity, and nonthought.

Bliss

There are two kinds of bliss. *Physical bliss* is at first mixed with the afflictions, but subsequently, bliss free from afflictions pervades the entire body. In the end, even if one feels heat, cold, and so on, the bliss is only intensified. With *mental bliss*, the mind becomes happy, joyful, and free from pain. This has the same three stages as in physical bliss.

Clarity

Clarity is also of two kinds. In the *clarity of the five senses*, the sign that the mind has become controlled is the appearance of what seem to be objects of visual perception: mirages, bright sparks that resemble fireflies, lamp flames, moons, suns, firelight, dots of light, rainbows, and a variety of beings and forms. In the *clarity of the mind*, as all thoughts of faults and their remedies arise, the mind, its manifestations, and their harmonious interdependence are known. And there is purity, clarity, freedom from sleepiness, and you think that you know all phenomena.

Nonthought

First you maintain the mind's focus upon any object. Then thoughts cease and your mind remains resting wherever it has been placed. In the end you experience the cessation of all thought activity.

When these experiences are accompanied by wisdom, you will know that *bliss* has no real nature, so that you will not be savoring its taste. *Clarity* will be free from the fault of becoming scattered and unstable through thoughts about causes and results. In *nonthought*, even though you've attained an unwavering state of mind, self-knowing will directly know the instantaneous arising and ceasing of mental activity. These are the signs that you are following the true path.

You will go astray if you become attached to the taste of the experience of bliss, if you become proud of clarity and believe in its perfection, and if, through experiencing the taste of nonthought blended with neutral emptiness, you start ignoring the law of karma. This may result in rebirth in the form realm, but this isn't the path to enlightenment. Therefore it's important that your experiences be accompanied by true wisdom.

There are many ways of going astray during this time, but they are all included in these three:

1. Emptiness becomes your enemy.
2. Compassion becomes your enemy.
3. Thoughts about cause and result become your enemy.

In the first, you think, "All phenomena are my mind. My mind is free of conceptual elaboration. Therefore nothing is real. So why should I make any effort with my body, speech, and mind? What is the point of doing composite good actions?" This is going astray as a result of emptiness becoming your enemy.

In the second, you think, "I must benefit beings through my compassion for all who don't have my kind of realization." Then, no longer listening to teachings or practicing, you abandon meditation and dedicate yourself to composite actions, exhausting yourself by your attachment to the reality of yourself and beings. This is going astray as a result of compassion becoming your enemy.

The third means that you see that everything is created by thought, and you think, "I shall make myself omniscient," and then practice the minor, ordinary activities of grammar, logic, crafts, and medicine, throwing aside the power of śamatha and vipaśyanā. This is going astray as a result of thoughts about cause and result becoming your enemy.

How you train with experiences

When you have the experience of bliss, seal it with emptiness and unreality. When thoughts manifest as clear appearances in the mind, enter into a clear and nonconceptual knowing. When you experience clairvoyance, the ten signs,[148] or other vivid perceptions of the five senses, be certain that they are nothing but your mind and have no attachment to their reality, fixating on their characteristics; instead, transcend it through your own freedom from conceptual elaboration.

When you experience nonthought and emptiness, seal it with the two experiences of clarity[149] and apply the analytic explanation of the causal and resultant interdependence, faults, and their remedies.

If while you are in solitude you experience that everything has blended into one taste, without any distinction between day or night, then blend happiness and suffering to see whether they become one taste or not.

If you feel proud of your experiences, know that it is the work of the māras and meditate on pure perception of everyone, developing compassion toward all beings, and developing an equanimity that will never have clinging attachment or rejecting aversion toward anything in samsara or nirvana.

Maximizing the results

You realize that the six consciousnesses and their six objects are nothing but your own mind and have no other creator. First you understand that perceiver and perceptions have no reality; then you experience it; and finally you see it directly.

It is important to identify the immediate mentation[150] of the arising and cessation of all consciousnesses. Whenever any of the six consciousnesses arise, they arise because of the mentation of "immediate activity," which when they cease, cause all good, bad, and meditation karma[151] to blend with the mind's ālaya consciousness. This is a secret that you should know.

Along with immediate mentation there arises "the afflicted mentation," which is the thought of "I," belief in a self, attachment to a self, and pride, which, because they obscure you, create ignorance. When the six consciousnesses develop upon that basis, subject and object are not recognized to be your own clarity, which creates thoughts of belief in the reality of the subject and object as "me and mine." This is how all afflictions are created.

It's taught that afflictions from the six consciousnesses, which are created by looking outward, are eliminated by the path of seeing,[152] while the afflictions created by looking inward are eliminated through the path of meditation.

Śrāvakas on the paths of seeing and meditation gain peace through eliminating the afflictions that come from only one aspect of the view that there is an individual self, but they are ignorant of "mental immediacy" and of its remedy—the selflessness of phenomena—and therefore they remain far from the great enlightenment of buddhahood.

Therefore a wise ordinary individual who has reached the mental state of dhyāna should meditate in the following way. When you rest in dhyāna without thoughts, the six consciousnesses cease in space. When you arise from that samādhi, you can see the movement of the subtle mental activity of thought. If at this time, you don't have the view taught by a true guru, you will have the following deluded thoughts:

You may have the nihilistic view, thinking, "There is no reality to the mind and no reality to its arising and ceasing, and therefore thoughts have no cause."

You may have the eternalistic view, thinking, "Even though thoughts themselves cease, they are permanent because they will always continue to arise and appear."

You may have thoughts about the self, thinking, "These movements of consciousnesses all occur within a single mind."

You may have the deluded thought that external objects should be stopped, thinking, "If I stopped the appearance of external objects, I would be in a state of nonthought, and so I must stop the appearances of objects."

You may go astray by thinking that dhyāna is the ultimate path, thinking, "The ultimate path is the dhyāna in which the activities of thought have ceased, in which joy and bliss have ceased, in which the movement of mindfulness and awareness has ceased, and in which the inhalation and exhalation of the breath have ceased."

You may go astray in a meditative state without identification, thinking, "The ultimate path is the nonconceptual clarity in which the identification that recognizes the characteristics of objects ceases."

You may go astray into the formless realm if you believe that the ultimate path is when all appearances and solidity cease into a consciousness that is like space, or into an infinite [consciousness], or into nothingness, or into the absence of both identification and nonidentification.[153]

This ignorance of the mind is the root of these and all other negative views in the three realms, such as that of belief in the individual self.[154] It is also the source of all afflictions. Therefore it is called the *afflicted mentation*. Its root is invalid conceptualization. When you have seen this, in the state of the clarity and nonthought of the external six consciousnesses, you will enter into wisdom.

The agitation of the mind's grasping at characteristics and engaging in acquiring and rejecting creates all the sufferings of samsara, while remedial knowledge creates all good karma and happiness in samsara. When you have understood this, mind, which thinks of and runs toward faults and remedies, should rest in meditation, in its own clarity and emptiness, and train in each of the four dhyānas, the four formlessnesses, and in cessation.

During post-meditation, understand and be skilled in all the ways in which all faulty and remedial thoughts create causes, conditions, and results. Know that all thoughts of identification through the triple aspects [of conceptualization] are obscurations. Seal all phenomena with impartiality, with their empty and selfless nature. Don't have the arrogance of seeing the mind, the ālaya, as "me and mine," but practice with diligence until all afflictions are purified and you have all thoughts under your power.

This is taught in detail in *Training Thoughts* and the *Four Connections*, so read those texts.[155]

> By becoming familiar with the direct nonconceptual knowledge
> of the clarity and nonthought of the six sensory consciousnesses,
> you will see the mind's self-knowing, direct mental perceptions,
> and the immediacy of mentation as being like the moon's reflection on water.

> Because of this the obscured ālaya
> and the unobscured mirror-like wisdom
> will see, in the manner of an inference, the true nature.

> Through remedies you will eliminate, transform, and realize the nature
> of both the obviously manifest and the latent afflictions.
> Then you will have mastery of pure discriminating wisdom
> with its samādhi, which realizes the elimination of both [manifest and latent afflictions].
> At that time, the ālaya will directly appear.

> The ālaya will be purified in the very instant that it is freed
> from all concepts concerning true nature and results,
> and at that time, you will attain the enlightenment of buddhahood.

Alas! Immature beings, who do not understand this
    nature,
bind themselves to "me and mine."
Those who are śrāvakas are bound
by the bondage of selflessness as a remedy.

Although training in concepts of phenomenal percepts
leads to the attainment of pratyekabuddhahood,
the perceiver aspect is not realized to be the ālaya,
so they remain on the path.

Complete buddhahood is total realization.
That is why buddhahood is unsurpassable.

Conclusion

While you are developing śamatha and vipaśyanā, agitating or
dulling thoughts may arise.

Recognize the causes of dullness and eliminate them by using
methods such as cooling yourself, bloodletting, directing your
awareness toward all your objects of perception, contemplating
cause and result, reading profound sutras, tantras, and treatises,
and then meditating.

If agitation or dispersal occurs, focus and control the breath,
because it is the steed of the mind; concentrate directly on an
object of meditation; examine yourself and meditate on the true
nature; and seal your meditation with the samādhi of bliss.

While practicing in this way and experiencing being free
from the two extremes, your behavior should transgress neither the rules of correct conduct nor your commitments. Thus
I say:

Have no doubt that the practitioner
who meditates upon this will gain realization.

Do not stop the conduct of realization
but rely on benefiting yourself and others.

Begin every session with taking refuge and developing bodhicitta and conclude them with a dedication for the benefit of all
beings throughout space, sealed with prayers of aspiration.

Glorious Tilopa has described the true nature of view, meditation, and action:

> The king of views is liberation from the margins
>   and extremes.
> The king of meditations is the absence of
>   distraction.
> The king of conduct is the absence of effort.
> The manifest result is the absence of hope and fear.[156]

Nāropa has also said:

> If your view is unmistaken in that way,
> you will attain enlightenment as fast as a race horse
> through your meditation and conduct
> truly being in accord with it.[157]

He also said:

> If you do not have the true view, you will gain noth-
> ing but meaningless exhaustion.[158]

He also said:

> If they are not in accord with the view,
> your meditation and conduct will be erroneous.
> Like a blind person without a guide,
> you will not reach the true result.[159]

The successive stages of mahāmudrā instructions are: The innate mahāmudrā that resides within you; the direct recognition of the meaning of the inseparability of appearance and emptiness; meditation on the inseparability of emptiness and compassion; the correct experience of śamatha and vipaśyanā; and the absence of mental activity within the nonconceptual meditation free from the five kinds of adverse factors.[160]

Rangjung Dorjé composed this slightly expanded version of a teaching by Kumāra Candraprabha[161] according to his own understanding, unmixed with words from academic texts.

> The Conqueror taught the profound path of innate
>   union
> in all his sutras and tantras.
> Tilopa and Nāropa summarized
> it as practice instructions,
> which their followers have taught.
>
> Some have taught in accordance with experience,
> while some have explained through conceptual analysis.
> It is not that all these teachings are not good,
> but they are only partial.
>
> Therefore here the meaning of innate union
> has been revealed—by words, meaning, and realization—
> as the wisdom that liberates all by knowing one thing.
>
> By the merit of this,
> may all beings realize the innate union.

This should be practiced in combination with the six Dharmas of Nāropa.

This was composed in Dechen[162] on the first day of the fifth month of the wood rat year (1324).

5. Prayer for the Definitive Meaning, the Mahāmudrā

Karmapa Rangjung Dorjé

This verse prayer by the Third Karmapa is the most widely known and taught text in this volume. Popularly called *The Mahāmudrā Prayer*, the *Prayer for the Definitive Meaning, the Mahāmudrā* has been translated elsewhere numerous times. Its popularity is due to its conciseness and because each four-line verse can be commented on separately. The translation here has been made according to the extensive commentary by the Eighth Situ Tenpai Nyinjé (1700–1777).[163]

Namo guru.

1. Gurus, deities of the *yidam* mandalas,
   conquerors and their children in the three times and ten
       directions,
   regard me with love and give me your blessing
   so that my prayer will be perfectly fulfilled.

2. May the rivers of accumulations of virtue, unpolluted by
       the triple aspects,
   that come from the snow mountains of the pure thoughts
       and actions
   of myself and all endless beings
   enter the ocean of the four kāyas.

3. Until the time that we attain that,
   may we throughout every lifetime
   never even hear the words "bad actions" and "suffering"
   and enjoy the glorious ocean of good actions and happiness.

4. May I obtain the supreme freedoms and wealths;
       have faith, diligence, and wisdom;
   rely on an excellent spiritual friend; obtain the quintes-
       sence of the teachings;
   practice them correctly and without any obstacle;
   and thus practice the sublime Dharma throughout all my
       lifetimes.

5. Hearing the scriptures and logic brings freedom from the
       clouds of ignorance.

Contemplating the instructions defeats the darkness of
   doubt.
The light of meditation illuminates the true nature, just as
   it is.
May the radiance of the three wisdoms increase.

6. The two truths, free from the two extremes of eternalism
     and nihilism, are the meaning of the basis.
   The two accumulations, free from the extremes of embel-
     lishment and denigration, are the supreme path.
   The attainment of the two benefits, free from the extremes
     of existence and peace, is the attainment of the result.
   May we meet this Dharma that is free of error.

7. The basis for purification is the mind—the union of clarity
     and emptiness.
   The purifier is the great vajra yoga of mahāmudrā.
   The purified are the stains of extrinsic delusion.
   May the result of purification, the stainless dharmakāya,
     become manifest.

8. The confidence of the view cuts through doubts about the
     basis.
   The essential point of meditation is to remain undistracted
     from that.
   The supreme conduct is training in the entire meaning of
     meditation.
   May there be the confidence of view, meditation, and
     conduct.

9. All phenomena are manifestations of the mind.
   The mind is without mind, devoid of an essence of mind,
   empty and unceasing, appearing as anything whatsoever.

May it be perfectly examined and be completely
   understood.

10. The self-appearances that have never existed are mistaken
       as objects.
    Through the power of ignorance, self-knowing is mistaken
       for a self.
    Through the power of dualism, we wander in the vastness
       of existence.
    May the error of ignorance be thoroughly understood.

11. It has no existence: even the conquerors have not seen it.
    It is not nonexistent: it is the basis for all samsara and
       nirvana.
    There is no contradiction: it is the path of the middle way,
       of union.
    May the true nature of the mind, free from extremes, be
       realized.

12. It cannot be indicated by saying, "It is this."
    It cannot be refuted by saying, "It is not this."
    The true nature that transcends the intellect is
       noncomposite.
    May there be certainty in the extreme of the true meaning.

13. If this is not realized, there will be circling within samsara.
    If this is realized, there is no other buddhahood.
    There is no "This is it; this isn't it" anywhere.
    May we know the true nature, the hidden secret of the
       ālaya.

14. Appearances are mind and emptiness is mind.
    Thoughts are mind and delusion is mind.
    Origination is mind and cessation is mind.

May we cut through all conceptual embellishments in the
   mind.

15. Unadulterated by mentally fabricated, forced meditation,
    unshaken by the winds of ordinary preoccupations,
    knowing how to naturally rest in unaltered naturalness—
    may we master and maintain the practice of the meaning
       of the mind.

16. The waves of obvious and subtle thoughts cease by
       themselves;
    the undisturbed river of the mind becomes naturally calm.
    May there be an untroubled peaceful sea of śamatha,
    free from the polluting impurities of dullness and
       agitation.

17. When we look again and again at the mind that cannot be
       seen,
    we will perfectly see that which is not seen, just as it is.
    May we cut through doubts as to what the meaning is or
       isn't
    and have unmistaken knowledge of our own nature.

18. Looking at objects, there are no objects: they are seen to be
       mind.
    Looking at the mind, there is no mind: it's devoid of
       essence.
    Looking at both spontaneously extinguishes dualism.
    May we realize luminosity, which is the nature of the
       mind.

19. The freedom from attention is the *mahāmudrā* (Great
    Seal).

The freedom from extremes is the *mahāmadhyamaka* (Great Middle Way).

This is also named the all-inclusive *dzokchen* (Great Perfection).

May there be the confidence that through knowing one all will be realized.

20. Continuous great bliss, free from attachment;
unveiled luminosity, free from fixation on attributes;
naturally present nonthought, transcending the intellect:
may there be a continuity of these effortless experiences.

21. Attachment to good and fixation on experiences is spontaneously liberated.
Bad thoughts and illusion are naturally purified in the element.
The ordinary mind has no rejection and adoption, no elimination and no attainment.
May we realize the truth of the true nature, free from conceptual elaborations.

22. The nature of beings is always buddhahood,
but not realizing that, they wander in endless samsara.
May I have overwhelming compassion
for beings in limitless, endless suffering.

23. When there is love with the unceasing power of overwhelming compassion,
the meaning of the empty essence appears nakedly.
May I meditate inseparably, day and night,
on the union, the supreme path, which is free from error.

24. Through the power of meditation, there is sight and clairvoyance,

beings are ripened, buddha realms are purified,
and the prayers for accomplishing the qualities of buddhahood are perfected.
May there be buddhahood, where perfection, ripening,
and fulfillment are brought to completion.

25. Through the compassion of the conquerors and their children in the ten directions,
and through the power of all the good karma there can be,
may my pure prayers, and those of all beings,
be perfectly fulfilled.

This *Prayer for the Definitive Meaning, the Mahāmudrā*, was
composed by the lord Karmapa Rangjung Dorjé.

6. The Bright Torch

The Perfect Illumination of the True Meaning of the
Mahāmudrā, the Essence of All the Dharma

⸻⸺⸺ ∞ ⸺⸺⸻

Tselé Natsok Rangdröl

Tselé Natsok Rangdröl (b. 1608) was a pupil of both the Sixth Shamarpa, Chökyi Wangchuk (1584–1630), and the Tenth Karmapa, Chöying Dorjé (1604–74). He was recognized as the rebirth of a lama as a child, and he had both Kagyü and Nyingma teachers. More than a meditation instruction, his *Bright Torch* presents mahāmudrā in terms of the three phases of basis, path, and result.[164] It categorizes the levels of enlightenment reached through mahāmudrā and relates those to the levels of bodhisattvas in general Buddhist teaching.

Namo mahāmudraye (Homage to mahāmudrā).

> I make an offering through the homage of perfectly
>   realizing
> the luminosity of the true nature, the supreme wisdom,
> the primordial, completely pure, natural state,
> which is devoid of all conceptual elaboration.
>
> I give this teaching so that we may recognize for ourselves
> the natural state of the innate inseparability
> of the apparent aspect, the variety of manifestations,
> and the essential aspect, their lack of any existence.

The essential meaning of all the infinite, endless teachings of all the conquerors is that the essence of a tathāgata's wisdom is present in the nature of beings. In order to reveal this, the conquerors teach countless, specific aspects or vehicles of the Dharma, within which there are as many different teachings and instructions as there are different aspirations and capabilities among pupils. This is the special, marvelous power of the compassionate activity of the buddhas.

Supreme among these teachings is mahāmudrā, which is as famous as the sun and moon. It is the fast path of the ultimate meaning, the summit of all the resultant Mantrayānas or Vajrayānas. It is the supreme method that easily and directly reveals the face of the mind's nature, the natural presence of the three kāyas. It is the single great path traveled by all the supreme siddhas and vidyādharas.

I will briefly teach the necessary essentials of its meaning in three parts. What are these three?

I. The basis mahāmudrā, which is the true nature of things: a brief teaching on the two aspects of delusion and liberation

II. The path mahāmudrā, which is self-arisen, natural resting: a detailed explanation of how a practitioner follows the path of śamatha and vipaśyanā

III. The result mahāmudrā, which is stainless true buddhahood: a conclusion that explains how beings are benefited by the manifestations of the three kāyas

I. The basis mahāmudrā

Samsara and nirvana have no real existence whatsoever. Their nature is without aspect or division, unstained by such terms as happiness or suffering, is or isn't, existent or nonexistent, eternalism or nihilism, self or other. Therefore it is free from all extremes of conceptual embellishment and has no existent essence. The key point is that it is the basis for any kind of appearance or characteristic to arise, but that whatever appears has no real existence.

This noncomposite dharmadhātu, the great emptiness free from the three extremes of arising, remaining, and ceasing, has primordially been the naturally present three kāyas. This is the basis, the true nature of things, which is called *mahāmudrā*. It is said in the *Secret Essence Tantra*:

> This mind, which is without root or basis,
> is the root of all phenomena.[165]

It is not like that in just one individual or in the mind continuum of just one buddha; it is the all-pervading basis for the entirety of all appearances and beings, all of samsara and nirvana.

Those who realize or know this true nature or identity are called *buddhas*. Those who do not realize or know it are deluded and are called *beings*. This is the basis for wandering in samsara.

Therefore it is known as the *basis of samsara and nirvana*. The Great Brahman Saraha has said:

> The mind alone is the seed of all.
> Samsara and nirvana emanate from it.[166]

Thus there is one essence with different aspects, and these aspects appear simply as a result of it being realized or not. However, the essence of these two aspects is the great primordial inseparability of the three kāyas, which is never polluted by faults such as [the duality of] good and bad, or change. Within the general vehicles this is called the *changeless absolute*.[167] This is the true nature of the primordial basis.

The true nature as a neutral impartiality, neither realized nor unrealized, is called the *ālaya* ("basis of everything") because it is the basis of both samsara and nirvana. The ālaya is not a total emptiness in which there is nothing. Rather, like a mirror and its clarity, there is an unimpeded self-illuminating knowing, which is called the *ālaya consciousness*.

THE WAY IN WHICH SAMSARA AND NIRVANA ARISE SEPARATELY FROM THIS SINGLE ĀLAYA

The knowing or wisdom aspect of self-illuminating cognition is the essence of the knowing that is an inseparability of the essence (which is emptiness) and the nature (which is clarity). It is the seed, or cause, of all the qualities of buddhahood and all the Dharmas of the true path. Therefore all the synonyms for nirvana correspond to it, such as the true ālaya, buddha nature, self-knowing, dharmakāya, perfection of wisdom, the buddhahood of one's own mind, and so on. This is what practitioners of the path have to directly perceive and recognize.

Alternatively, the dullness aspect of the neutral ālaya is not knowing oneself: that is to say, obscuring oneself through not knowing one's true nature. This is called *innate ignorance*, the *great darkness of beginningless time*, and also the *ālaya of diverse propensities*, as all afflictions and deluded thoughts arise because of it. It is the basis for the delusion of all beings. It is said in the *Tantra of the Unimpeded View*:

> When knowing does not arise in the basis,
> there is a dull mindlessness.
> This is the cause of ignorance and delusion.[168]

Accompanying this ignorance, as a kind of retinue, are the seven kinds of thought that arise from ignorance, such as medium attachment and forgetfulness.

The conception of an "I" or self arises from that innate ignorance, and that causes the conception of others in relation to the self. Appearances coming from you are not recognized to be coming from you but are conceived of as external objects. That is how delusion begins: by not recognizing the concepts of subject and object for what they are. This is *conceptual ignorance*. It is also called *mental consciousness*. It is the deluded mind that creates the separation between mind and objects. It has a retinue of forty kinds of thoughts, such as craving and grasping, that arise from desire. This mental consciousness has the power to create and multiply a variety of propensities and delusions. It is aided by karmic wind as a pervasive condition and the ālaya's causal ignorance. The developing power of factors of dependent origination such as these—the triad of body, appearances, and mind—are completely created. The arising of five distinct sense consciousnesses and the thoughts and perceptions of all six sense consciousnesses is what is called the *dependent*.[169]

The five major root winds, the five minor branch winds, and the rest serve as steeds for thoughts. At the same time habituation to being fixated on delusion causes the appearances that come from yourself to appear to be the world and its inhabitants. Thus this forms both the foundational basis and its object and gives rise to everything. This is what is called the *afflicted mind*. It is also called the *consciousnesses of the five senses*, because it creates attachment and so on through each of the five sensory organs. This is accompanied by thirty-three thoughts that arise from anger, such as medium nonattachment.[170] The ālaya and its diverse propensities are the roots, and the eighty kinds of thoughts have the nature of being branches. This is a sequential development that forms the unbroken continuum of delusion that causes you to wander endlessly in samsara. That is how beings without realization are deluded.

The propensities for every phenomena of samsara and nirvana are present in the form of seeds within the ālaya. They are the cause of the appearance, through a process of dependent origination, of all internal substances (the evident material body and also its various channels, winds, and drops, and its purities and impurities) and all external substances (the worlds and beings of the three realms of samsara and nirvana). These do not truly exist but are relative, illusory appearances, just like whatever appears in a dream. Extremely strong habituation to the belief that they are permanent, and to attachment to solidity and reality, causes the experience of the various states of happiness, suffering, and neutrality within the three realms and the six classes of beings. Thus the causes and results of samsara cycle continuously and naturally, like a water wheel. That is the general characteristics of beings, but even while they are deluded and wandering in samsara, all these obscurations cannot cause even an atom's worth of degeneration in the element of buddha nature, which is the essence of knowing. It is said in the *Hevajra Tantra*:

> All beings are indeed buddhas
> but are obscured by extrinsic impurities.[171]

Ultimately, the primordial true nature is brilliant since it is the inseparability of the three kāyas. Even during the intermediate period, when the extrinsic stains of illusory appearances obscure it, its own nature is as radiant as the three kāyas. In the end, too, when the obscurations have been cleared away and the result of developing the two wisdoms has been made manifest, it shines as the three kāyas.

Therefore the terms *liberation* and *illusion* signify only whether there is freedom from the stains of ignorance and illusory thought or not. It is said in the *Sublime Continuum*:

> As it was before, so it is afterward.
> It has the quality of changelessness.[172]

Therefore the mind naturally has a primordially pure essence. The extrinsic illusions or innate ignorance are like discolorations forming on gold, arising from itself and obscuring itself. [The Buddha] taught a variety of distinct methods for its cleansing and purification, but the mind's essence is the aspect of wisdom itself, the self-arising wisdom that remains unchanged throughout the three times and is free from conceptual elaboration. Thus the ultimate viewpoint of the Conqueror is that method and wisdom includes all paths.

You might ask, "But how can samsara and nirvana possibly be divisions of this single ālaya?" The answer is that camphor as a medicine can be either beneficial or harmful according to whether the illness is a hot or a cold illness. A poisonous substance can be transformed into medicine by certain methods, such as mantras, but it will kill you if you take it without those methods. In the same way, you will be liberated if you know and recognize the two essences of the ālaya, but you will be deluded if you do not and instead conceive of a self. This difference is simply the result of having or not having realization. Ārya

Nāgārjuna has said:

> Those who are caught in the net of afflictions
> are those who are called *beings*.
> Those who are free from the afflictions
> are those who are called *buddhas*.[173]

Therefore, if you follow the instructions on mahāmudrā, which is the definitive meaning and the essence of the entire Dharma, you will attain the true nature itself, which is the *basis mahāmudrā*. The *path mahāmudrā* purifies you of the stains of illusory thoughts, and the *result mahāmudrā* is gaining the kingdom of the three kāyas. As this opens the treasury of the two benefits, worthy and prepared individuals should seek out a guru with the necessary qualities and the quintessential blessing. They should follow him as described in the accounts of Sudhana and Sadāprarudita[174] or in the biographies of Tilopa and Nāropa.

You definitely need to be ripened by the stages of a ripening [empowerment], whatever its degree of nonelaboration or elaboration. That is the principal entranceway into the Vajrayāna path. Until you have obtained the signs [of accomplishment], dedicate yourself, without being perfunctory, idle, or indifferent, to all the general and special preliminaries, which are highly valued as leading to the liberating instructions.

In particular, dedicate yourself to the sincere practice of guru-yoga devotion, which will definitely bring the power of blessing to you. That is the essence of the practice of all Kagyü siddhas and vidyādharas. It is said in the *Essence of a Precious Portion of the Tantras*:

> This innate wisdom, which is beyond description,
> is solely the result of gathering the accumulations, purifying the obscurations,
> and receiving the blessing of a realized guru.

> Know that those who rely on other methods are
> foolish.[175]

As for the main practice, there are different traditions, with some recognizing meditation through the view, some gaining certainty in view through meditation, and so on. Whichever tradition you follow, the main important thing is receiving the blessing of the guru and lineage.

As for the view, there are countless ways of teaching it in the different philosophical traditions and vehicles, and each of them has established its own view as being true. All these vehicles are countless, infinite doorways established by activity of the Conqueror, and therefore I don't declare one to be correct and another not, one good and another bad; instead I rejoice in them all.

The view that I will explain here is that the nature of the mind is a primordial, naturally present, great, complete purity. It is free from the elaborations of coming and going, arising, remaining, and ceasing in the three times of the past, future, and present. It is unpolluted by the concepts of samsara, nirvana, and the path. It does not have the conceptual embellishments of existence or nonexistence, being or not being, eternalism or nihilism, good or bad, high or low, and so on. It does not have cessation or creation, rejection or adoption, transformation or establishment of any phenomena within the appearances and existences that are samsara and nirvana.

This primordial state or quality has the nature of the vivid inseparability of appearance and emptiness; the radiant unity of clarity and emptiness; the brilliant, all-pervading, primordial liberation; and bright, noncomposite natural presence. This is the primordial, self-arising nature of the principal view. It is the primordial, all-pervading essence of samsara and nirvana. Any other view is partial, fragmentary, and biased.

Knowing the falsehood of dualism through knowing this

primordial nature is called *realizing the view, seeing the mind,* and *knowing the meaning of phenomena.* It is said in *Treasury of Dohas*:

> When you have realized it, it is everything.
> There is nothing else for anyone to know.[176]

Ultimately all the phenomena of appearances and existences, of samsara and nirvana, are the display of the three kāyas. Even your own mind has the nature of the three kāyas. The three kāyas too are not outside the essential element that is the ultimate true nature.

All the phenomena of samsara are the characteristics of the mind. All Dharmas of the path are the qualities of the mind, and all the qualities of the result are the power of the mind.

The mind's unborn nature is the dharmakāya. The mind's unimpeded clarity is the saṃbhogakāya. The mind's power to appear as anything is the nirmāṇakāya. Those three are naturally present as an inseparable essence. Gaining certainty through recognizing this nature is called the *faultless, unmistaken view* and *true realization.*

Any other view with concepts, such as of being liberated or not being liberated from the extremes, of being high or low, or of being good or bad—any view or meditation in which mental fabrication and analysis create concepts—will not be the view of mahāmudrā.

II. The path mahāmudrā, which is self-arisen, natural resting: a detailed explanation of how a practitioner follows the path of śamatha and vipaśyanā

This teaching includes śamatha, vipaśyanā, faults and qualities, meditation and post-meditation, how the practitioner should follow the path, and so on.

[A. Śamatha]

Generally, the word *meditation* can refer to many things. There are countless methods of meditation in the different traditions, but here the word or term *meditation* refers solely to internal familiarization with the natural state—that is, to the view that has just been explained. It does not signify a mentally contrived meditation on things with color and shape, or meditation on an artificial emptiness where all the mind's movements, thoughts, appearances, and perceptions have ceased. Here meditation is solely maintaining your mind just as it is, without creating anything.

Specifically, there are varying capacities or minds. There are "immediate" individuals who have sharp faculties and evidently have trained in their past lives. They don't need to be guided through sequential stages of śamatha and vipaśyanā because they become liberated immediately on their direct introduction [to the nature of the mind].

However, ordinary people need to be guided in stages. They begin with training in śamatha on an object such as a twig, a pebble, a deity's image, a syllable, a quintessence (*bindu*), or the breath. When they have gained stability in those practices, they practice supreme, objectless śamatha. This is true śamatha, and it is taught through three methods:

1. The mind rests in a fresh and undistracted state, in which it is not distracted by any internal or external object.
2. The three doors rest effortlessly, naturally, and loosely, without being very tightly controlled.
3. There is no separation or division, as when applying a remedy, between mindful knowing and the essence of thoughts. Instead there is just resting in the mind's self-knowing, self-clarity, and self-purity.

These three are also known as *nondistraction*, *nonmeditation*, and *nonfabrication*.

These also include the three doors of liberation taught within the general vehicles:

1. The door of liberation called *signlessness* is when the mind is not concerned with past activities, with thoughts about what was done or what happened, and so on.

2. The door of liberation called *emptiness* is when the present mind performs no mental modifications, neither creating nor stopping anything because of thinking that something has appeared or something needs to be done.

3. The door of liberation named *no aspiration* is [the mind] not thinking forward to what may happen in the future and having no expectations, such as hoping to be able to meditate or worrying about not being able to meditate.

These can be briefly summarized into just resting the mind naturally, as it is, unpolluted by alteration.

When a thought suddenly appears within that state, it is enough to simply be clearly aware of it, without becoming involved with it. Don't try to stop the thought in any way. Don't try to bring back meditation or apply some other remedy. Anything like that isn't the key point for maintaining an unaltered, unfabricated mind.

There are various teachings in other different paths, but this is the path of simply recognizing whatever arises. Any other method you use will not be mahāmudrā meditation. The Great Brahman has said:

> Beings are polluted by seeking meditation.
> There is nothing at all on which to meditate.
> A single instant of being without any yearning.
> That is the meditation of mahāmudrā.[177]

When directly resting in the nature of mind as it is, the

experiences of the three states of śamatha will sequentially arise. What are they?

THE FIRST [ŚAMATHA]

There will be brief periods when the mind appears to be wilder, with more thoughts than ever before. Don't think that producing these thoughts is a fault, for there has never been anything but this production [of thoughts]; it's just that you were not aware of them. When you become aware of the difference between the mind at rest and the mind producing thoughts, you will have reached the first śamatha, which is like a waterfall.

[THE SECOND ŚAMATHA]

As a result of maintaining that first śamatha, most of your thoughts will be subdued and move gently. Your body and mind will feel comfortable. You will be attracted to meditation and have no longing to engage in other activities. Most of the time, you will have a powerful stability without any movement or production of thoughts. This is the intermediate śamatha, which is said to be like the slow flow of a great river.

[THE THIRD ŚAMATHA]

If you continue to practice diligently, without distraction, you will reach a state where your body will have intense bliss with no sensation of pain. Your mind will have an unblemished purity and clarity that transcends the afflictions, which are no longer experienced. For as long as you meditate, you will be unwavering, with nothing being able to disturb you. Obvious afflictions will cease. You will have little attachment to food, clothes, and so on. You will have various experiences of limited clairvoyance and visions. You will gain many such general "qualities." That is the ultimate śamatha, which is like an unmoving ocean.

There have been many meditators with strong dedication but little learning and without an experienced teacher who during this stage became proud of these outward qualities. Then people believed them to be siddhas, which proved disastrous for others as well as themselves. So be careful this doesn't happen to you.

It's been taught that the practice of śamatha alone cannot be the true practice of mahāmudrā, but as it is its foundation, it is truly of great importance. Gyalwa Lorepa has said:

> Even if you meditate for a long time in a relaxed śamatha
> that is devoid of clarity, you will not realize the meaning.
> Meditate with the sharpness of knowing's gaze
> in a continuity of successive short sessions.[178]

B. The main practice: vipaśyanā

You need to investigate, until doubts are eradicated, whether the nature of the mind has truly existing characteristics, such as shape and color, and whether it has arising, abiding, and going; birth and cessation; or existence or nonexistence; whether it is eternal or nothing; has edges or a center; and so on. If you do not do that, you will not gain the actual view, and therefore you will not know how to maintain natural resting, natural meditation. Then, however dedicated you are to controlling your mind, your śamatha will be stupid and forced, and you will never transcend the karma of samsara's three realms. Therefore, with a genuine teacher, you must eradicate your misconceptions. In particular, as you are a practitioner of the Mantrayāna, the path of blessing, devote yourself to devotional prayers, dedicating yourself to the method for receiving the lineage's blessing for realization.

When you do that, your own knowing will be the natural presence of the primordial dharmakāya, as previously described in the description of the view. It is a nonconceptual, directly experienced wisdom that does not fall into any extreme, such as existence or nonexistence, being or not being, eternalism or nihilism. Although you will know and experience the inseparability of clarity, knowing, and emptiness, you will have no example to give for it and no way to express it in words. This clear, self-arising self-illumination is called *vipaśyanā*.

At first, while you're still an ordinary being, although it's never apart from you for even an instant, you fail to recognize it because you haven't received the instructions and the blessing. In the intermediate period, it is what rests in śamatha, what sees and knows whether you are at rest or not, and so on, but though it is all this, it does not see itself. The continuous production of thoughts in the ordinary state is nothing other than this vipaśyanā itself appearing as thoughts. The experience of śamatha and of bliss, clarity, and nonthought are nothing but the arising of this vipaśyanā's knowing.

If you do not know your own naked nature, free from thought, you will have mental stability only, which cannot be a cause of enlightenment. Once you have seen your own nature, all mental stillness or production will be nothing other than vipaśyanā or mahāmudrā. Lorepa has said:

> Do not engage in mental fixation upon
> anything that appears to the six consciousnesses.
> Everything is self-appearing and self-liberating.
> All you meditators, have you realized this
> inseparability?[179]

In general, it is said:

> Śamatha is when thoughts cease of themselves and
> the mind rests in clarity, bliss, and nonthought.
> Vipaśyanā is clearly seeing the naked nature of the
> mind as self-illuminating, objectless, and without
> embellishment.[180]

It is also taught:

> Alternatively, śamatha is freedom from the production and dissolution of thoughts, while vipaśyanā is the recognition of that process itself.[181]

There are many such statements, but their meaning is that whatever appears, whatever arises, is nothing other than the inseparability of śamatha and vipaśyanā. All [mental] stillness and movement is nothing other than the play of the mind itself. Therefore, if you have this recognition during either stillness or movement, that is vipaśyanā.

Śamatha is when there is no attachment to solidity in relation to any external appearance to the six consciousnesses. Vipaśyanā is the unimpeded appearance of whatever arises in the mind. Therefore appearances possess the complete union of vipaśyanā and śamatha.

Śamatha is the clear awareness of a thought as it vividly arises. Vipaśyanā is when that thought is liberated within the naked, intellect-free mind. Therefore thoughts, too, contain the union of vipaśyanā and śamatha.

Śamatha is when you do not perceive the arising of intense afflictions as solid but see instead their very nature. Vipaśyanā is naked clarity and emptiness in which there is no separation between the seer's knowing and the seen afflictions. Therefore in afflictions also you find the complete union of vipaśyanā and śamatha.

In brief, there is no stillness or movement, emanation or absorption, or good or bad within the nature of the mind. All those appearances are simply its unimpeded power of display. Śamatha and vipaśyanā, too, are simply that kind of inseparable union. Nevertheless, to make it easier for people to engage in their different aspects, there is the teaching of their having separate names and categories.

The reason why it's said that śamatha alone is not true mahāmudrā meditation is that mental stability alone is only a mundane teaching. It's the same as the dhyānas of the tīrthikas, the Buddhist śrāvakas and pratyekabuddhas, and the samādhis of the deva realms. It is not the genuine path of the Mantrayāna's fourth empowerment, and it especially cannot be mahāmudrā if there is any attachment to the experience of mental stability, because in mahāmudrā, all appearances and existences become the path of the dharmakāya. If the mind's stillness is practiced and its movement is avoided, with one seen as good and the other bad, with one seen as meditation and the other not, then appearances and existences will not be the dharmakāya. Rather, practice where everything that appears, without any alteration, *is* the mahāmudrā.

Having briefly described what śamatha and vipaśyanā mean, I now give a brief description of faults, qualities, and possible errors. This has two parts:

1. The general errors of not knowing how to maintain meditation
2. Various specific errors and blunders and how to eliminate them

1. The general errors of not knowing how to maintain meditation

Resting in the unaltered mind is the essential meaning of all the countless, profound, and vast meditation instructions, such as mahāmudrā, dzokchen, result as the path (*lamdré*), severance (*chö*), and pacification (*shiché*). Nevertheless these different kinds of instructions exist because individuals differ in their understanding.

Some meditators say that meditation is simply the nonconceptual knowledge that all the obvious and subtle perceptions of the six consciousnesses have ceased, but this is just relaxed śamatha. Some arrogantly assume that their meditation is stable when there is a neutral state of dullness devoid of aware mindfulness. Some state that meditation is a state of mind that has perfect clarity, vivid bliss, and utter emptiness, but this is merely being fixated on meditation experiences. Some say that all meditation is simply the blank consciousness that comes between the cessation of one thought and the arising of the next, but that is fragmentary meditation. Some say that meditation is maintaining such thoughts as "The mind is the dharmakāya. It is empty. It is ungraspable," or "Nothing has any reality. Everything is like an illusion, like space," and so on, but this is falling into the extreme of mental fabrication and mental analysis. Some say that meditation is just whatever you think of, whatever comes up in the mind, but this is to fall under the power of ordinary thoughts, which brings the danger of insanity. Most others say that the mind's movements are faults that must be stopped, that you rest in meditation by restraining the mind's movement, but this is having a mindfulness that is too strict and too tight, which results in an uncomfortable mental bondage.

In brief, whether your mind is still or in movement, whether you have intense thoughts and afflictions or are in a vivid state of bliss, clarity, or nonthought, whatever is happening, there is no need for fabrication, alteration, elimination, or transformation. You only need to maintain a natural, innate process. In these times, when there are very few who know this, we need a faultless practice that accords with the actual view taught in the collected works, practice instructions, and manuals of the siddha lineages and in the sutras and tantras that teach the definitive meaning.

2. Various specific errors and blunders

The past masters in the practice lineage taught extensively and in detail about these errors and mistakes, whereas I will describe them here in just a few token sentences.

Attachment to experiences of clarity, bliss, or nonthought in your meditation will cause rebirth in the desire, form, or formless realms. When that life ends, you will fall into the lower existences, where you will no longer be on the path to buddhahood.

We can examine this process in detail through the specifics of the nine dhyānas of concentration:

1. When you can rest in śamatha without any obvious thoughts of subject and object but are still constrained by belief in there being a meditator and meditation, this is called the *first dhyāna's samādhi*, because this is how the devas in the first dhyāna realms meditate. Therefore meditating in this way will cause you to be reborn as a first-dhyāna deva.

2. In the second dhyāna you do not analyze or examine with your thoughts, but you nevertheless are experiencing the flavor of blissful samādhi.

3. In the third dhyāna, your mind is unwavering, dependent solely upon the inhalation and exhalation of the breath.

4. The fourth dhyāna is a samādhi that is devoid of all thought and has a space-like unobstructed clarity.

Although those [four dhyānas] are renowned to be the highest among all mundane samādhis and are a basis for vipaśyanā, to meditate on them with attachment will be an error in mahāmudrā, causing rebirth as a dhyāna deva. There are also [the dhyānas of]:

5. Thinking "All phenomena are infinite like space."

6. Thinking "This consciousness is not limited. It is infinite."

7. Thinking "There is neither identification nor the absence of identification, so that the mind has no activity."

8. Thinking "This mind is empty. It is nothing whatsoever."

Resting in those four levels [of dhyāna] has the defect of straying into the four kinds of formless abodes: *infinite space, infinite consciousness, neither existence nor nonexistence*, and *nothingness*.

9. The śrāvaka's samādhi of peace: This is the state of mind in which all those thoughts are eliminated, all engagement with objects has ceased, and there is a stability in which both mind and breath's movements have ceased.

That is taught to be the ultimate śamatha, but if it's devoid of vipaśyanā, it's not what is meant here by faultless meditation.

Each of those nine concentration dhyānas have only the qualities of accomplishing such things as the clairvoyance or miraculous powers of their level, but you must also know that according to this teaching, let alone the ultimate goal of complete buddhahood, they don't even accomplish the relative, apparent qualities. Even if they do incidentally accomplish them, if that causes attachment and pride, they will truly be obstacles to enlightenment.

Having explained those errors and wrong paths, I will now teach the *eight failings*.

1. *The primordial failing in relation to the nature of emptiness*: This is not realizing the mind to "have the supreme of all aspects," a term that means the unity of appearance and emptiness as an unimpeded interdependence of causes and results. Instead your focus is on emptiness alone. You must know this to be a defect.

2. *The circumstantial failing in relation to the nature [of emptiness]*: This is meditating with a comprehension of the meaning but without the experience of it having arisen within you—or you forget whatever experience you've had—so that while you can explain the meaning to others, you don't have it within yourself.

3. *The primordial failing in relation to the path*: This is thinking that what you need now is the path while the result is something else that will be obtained later.

4. *The circumstantial failing in relation to the path*: This is thinking that simply maintaining the "ordinary mind"—

your own mind—is not enough. Instead you seek elsewhere for some longed-for, imagined, marvelous meditation.

5. *The primordial failing in relation to remedies*: This is not realizing that when something like an affliction arises, that itself should be brought onto the path. Instead you meditate by using other methods from the lower vehicles.

6. *The circumstantial failing concerning remedies*: This is not knowing that when something like a thought arises, it should be used as the path. Instead you think that you must stop or destroy these factors in order to be in meditation.

7. *The primordial failing concerning the seal of emptiness*: This is not understanding that the mind is primordially empty, without any root. Instead you apply a seal of emptiness, such as a mentally fabricated emptiness or a transitory emptiness, by such thoughts as "This has no existing nature" or "This becomes empty."

8. *The circumstantial failing concerning the seal [of emptiness]*: This is continually thinking such thoughts as, "I used to be involved in thoughts, but now I meditate well." Or it's having no aware mindfulness but thinking that you do have it and so on.

To sum up, cutting through conceptual embellishment about the nature of things and knowing the flaws concerning the true nature are the key factors without which you will be in danger of falling into these similitudes of meditation; and all kinds of other things can happen too. However much effort you put into these similitudes of meditation, you will just tire yourself out to no purpose. Some even create the cause and conditions for a bad rebirth (such as meditation on a śamatha of "cessation" causing rebirth as a nāga). Therefore it's very important that your meditation be without error.

Also, there are those who are attached to a dull, dim state of mind without thought, believing it to be śamatha. There are those who are proud of their conceptual examination and analysis, believing it to be vipaśyanā. There are those whose goal is a mindfulness that clings tightly to the solidity of existence. There are those who mistake a neutral equanimity for the unaltered state. There are those who mistake the common ordinary mind, which does not see the actual face of the true nature, for the unaltered, unfabricated, intrinsic "ordinary" mind. There are those who become attached to a good samādhi. There are those who believe that mere stained bliss, which is free of pain, is the natural supreme bliss. There are those who have not reached certainty in the recognition of objectless true nature and instead mistake fixation on a perceived object for the fixation-free, objectless, unceasing, natural clarity. And there are those who mistake mental dullness that is due to the cessation of clarity for nonconceptual wisdom.

C. A summary of the cause of every kind of error, similitude, mistake, and failing

In the beginning, there is the error of not purifying the stains of bad karma because of not properly engaging in the preliminaries, such as gathering the accumulations and purifying the obscurations.

In the intermediate period, there is the fault of having a mind that is coarse and stiff because it has not been moistened by blessing. There is also the error of becoming intractably focused on words and verbal Dharma because the main practice hasn't cut through conceptual embellishments in your mind.

In the end, you become unable to assimilate practice and are just a yellow-clad person belonging to neither this world nor the Dharma, or you will be just a merchant in the teachings of the practice lineage. There are plenty of people like that in this final stage of the era of degeneration. It is said in the *Ten Wheels of Kṣitigarbha Sutra*:

Those who are Cārvāka tīrthikas
do not believe in the ripening of karma.
As soon as they die, they are reborn in Avīci hell.
They cause the ruin of others and also destroy
    themselves.[182]

It's important to make an effort to be in control of yourself so
that you don't end up like that. Apply yourself single-mindedly
to meditation without falling under the power of the errors and
failings in view and meditation. The "subsequent knowledge"
[of post-meditation] should also be in the grip of mindfulness
and awareness, so that you don't inattentively remain in ordinary
illusions. If you can do this, you will have experiences and realization according to your individual mentality and capability.

[D. Meditation and post-meditation]

Generally, scholars and siddhas have given numerous distinct
teachings on meditation and post-meditation at this level, so
that there are many different ways of identifying them. Some
teach that in the four yogas there is no actual teaching on meditation and post-meditation below the level of nonelaboration.
Some make a distinction between "realization's meditation
and post-meditation" and "experience's meditation and post-
meditation." Some teach easily perceived forms of meditation
and post-meditation as distinct in each of the four yogas. There
are innumerable teachings like this and, similarly, a variety of
explanations on the difference between experience and realization. Some teach that all three levels of one-pointedness have
only experience and no true realization. Some teach that when
you have the true meditation [of one-pointedness], you see the
essence of the mind. There seem to be innumerable subtle clas-
sificatory teachings like this. They manifest from the compassionate wish for methods that will train the countless different

dispositions and natures that individuals have. Therefore I have no doubt that they are all true, and I take refuge in them all. I don't have the training, insight, and knowledge of that level, so if I were to give reasons why some are right and some are wrong, I'd be no different than a blind person trying to distinguish between good and bad colors.

Nevertheless, to briefly describe what I have been able to understand, *meditation* and *post-meditation* are terms or signifiers used in the practice of both [the generation and completion] stages. *Meditation* is concentration on the actual practice without being mixed with any other kind of activity. The term *post-meditation* is used for when the practice is mixed with other activities during the period in between sessions and so on. Its knowledge is called *subsequent knowledge*, and its "appearances" are called *subsequent appearances*. This use of these terms is agreed upon by all. In this teaching, *meditation* is used for when beginners are engaged in actual meditation, and *post-meditation* is used for when they are doing things, moving around, walking, eating, sleeping, and so on. However, when higher practitioners are completely free of delusion, they are said to have "inseparable meditation and post-meditation" or "ceaseless meditation."

Similarly, to make a distinction between experience and realization, they are, respectively, like a fault and a remedy in a practice that is not blended with the nature of the mind, at whatever level it may be. *Experience* is when the meditator and the meditation appear to be separate. *Realization* is gaining complete certainty that they are not separate from the mind but that it is the mind itself that arises as their natures. In brief, these two occur not only in meditation but in most practices of the path, such as guru yoga, compassion, bodhicitta, and the generation stage. For example, *comprehension* is like hearing from others a description of the shape and layout of Bodhgaya so that you get a general impression of it in your mind that you can also relate to others. *Experience* is like seeing Bodhgaya from a distance or looking at a painting of its layout, so that you comprehend most of what there is to be known about it. *Realization* is like arriving at Bodhgaya and having the certainty of seeing it in all its details.

[E. How the practitioner should follow the path]

The way in which meditation and post-meditation are introduced into the mind depends on which of three levels of capability an individual is on. The immediate individuals are great beings who make their previous training evident; they have immediate comprehension, experience, and realization the moment they are shown a symbol, and without difficulty or effort they perfect these qualities. Medium individuals are of the "nonsequential" type. They are those for whom qualities of realization don't arise in a fixed order but are unpredictably high or low and may increase or decrease. Gradualist individuals are ordinary beings who progress, depending on their diligence, through a definite sequence of common, general practices.

The graduated path for gradualist individuals includes the other two paths, so I will explain that.

The common vehicles teach that you reach buddhahood by traversing the general ten levels and the five paths, but the unequaled Dakpo Kagyü succession of gurus and pupils teaches the particular four stages of yoga, each one divided into greater, lesser, and medium levels, making twelve. Lord Kumāra Candraprabha explained this to be the view of the *Tantra of the Inconceivable Secret*.[183] That tantra says:

> The samādhi of the awesome lion awakens
> pure, unwavering, one-pointed knowledge
> from within self-knowing wisdom.
> The stable *patience* eradicates the suffering of the lower
>   existences.

Second, through the samādhi that is like an illusion,
inconceivable samādhi arises as power
from the great meditation of nonelaboration.
Heat is attained and there is control over birth.

Third, the samādhi that is heroic
causes the realization of the one taste of multiplicity to
    arise.
You are a child of the buddhas of the three times and
    benefit others.
The *summit* is attained and there is continuous
    development.

Fourth, through application to the practice of
    nonmeditation,
which is the samādhi that is like a vajra,
there is the knowledge of wisdom and the Buddha realms
    are seen.
There is the unsought, naturally present state of the great
    supreme quality.

This viewpoint is taught extensively in the *Laṅkāvatāra Sutra*,
and it has also been clearly explained by Ācārya Śāntipa, who
made classifications such as the five kinds of vision and omniscience. Guru Rinpoché also taught this in brief in the Nyingma
tradition's mahāmudrā teachings, in the *Record of Key Points*,
which combines the four yogas with the four eliminations. One-
pointed [yoga is explained by the lines]:

Good and bad actions are purified in the mind
so that bad actions are naturally eliminated.

Nonelaboration:

> The elaboration-free nature of the mind
> eliminates all subjects and objects.

One taste:

> Appearances arise as the dharmakāya
> so that thoughts are spontaneously eliminated.

Nonmeditation:

> Samsara and nirvana are known to have no real nature,
> so that all dualism is eliminated.

It also teaches the view that the four yogas correspond with the *four certainties* of the path of engagement and so on:

> *Heat* is seeing the essence of the mind.
> *Summit* is realizing the birthless dharmakāya.
> *Patience* is having neither samsara nor nirvana, neither
>   adoption nor rejection.
> The *supreme quality* is samsara and nirvana dissolving
>   into the mind.[184]

I will now give a seed-like description of:
  1. The meaning of the four yogas
  2. The way in which the four yogas arise in sequence
  3. A supplement that explains how the sutra tradition's paths
     and stages are completely included within the four yogas

1. The meaning of the four yogas

This has four parts: one-pointed yoga, nonelaboration, one taste, and nonmeditation.

a. One-pointed yoga

LESSER ONE-POINTED YOGA

Capable individuals who can cut through attachment to this life, see the guru as truly being a buddha, and truly receive blessing will, when resting in meditation, abide in states of clarity, bliss, and nonthought. They will attain stability and certainty. Their thoughts will be spontaneously liberated as they recognize them. This will be accompanied by the fixation of thinking "This is meditation."

Past practice-lineage masters taught that all three levels of one-pointed yoga were solely śamatha. However, in my understanding, there are some definite differences between individuals on these different levels. There are others who view these levels as being within the province of vipaśyanā because the single knowledge of the true nature always has the inherent quality of being a union of śamatha and vipaśyanā.

At this level, the "subsequent knowledge" predominantly perceives things as real, and the practitioner's sleep is no different from that of an ordinary person. In brief, as this is the initial stage, there will be various degrees of ease and difficulty to maintaining the practice.

MEDIUM ONE-POINTED YOGA

During this stage, you are able to remain in meditation for as long as you wish. Samādhi will even arise sometimes when you're not meditating. Your "subsequent knowledge" will have a diminution of belief in reality, and appearances become spacious and clear. You can even at times practice while asleep. In brief, during this stage, whenever you meditate, you *will* be meditating.

GREATER ONE-POINTED YOGA

It's taught that there will be a constant experience, day and night, of bliss, clarity, and nonthought. There will be no distinct "subsequent appearances," "subsequent knowledge," and so on, as they will always be within samādhi. You will have no external or internal parasites. You will have no attachment to sensory pleasures. You will attain clairvoyance, miraculous powers, and so on. However, you will still not be free from attachment to good experiences, and you will not yet be liberated from the bondage of your mind's fixation on meditation. Therefore there can be many individual variations because of such factors as someone's diligence or level of capability for engaging in these three stages of one-pointed yoga.

Seeing the essence of one-pointed yoga is dependent on attaining the confidence that comes from the certainty of self-knowing in the very essence of bliss, clarity, and nonthought. Similarly, attaining mastery depends on your experiences being continuous. "Thoughts arising as meditation" depends on simply training in mindfulness of every thought that arises. The "arising of qualities" depends on your mind becoming tractable. Planting the seed of the form kāyas depends on uncontrived compassion arising during "subsequent knowledge." Fully understanding relative truth depends on certainty in the interdependence of causes and results. Past Kagyü masters have taught that we must know these categories.

b. Nonelaboration yoga

Whatever experiences you have in one-pointed yoga, if you can apply yourself to practice and prayer without falling under the power of the arrogant belief in a self and attachment to good experiences, then you will progress to the yoga of nonelaboration.

LESSER NONELABORATION

You truly realize that the mind has no extremes of arising, remaining, and ceasing. When you have mindfulness, your "subsequent knowledge" is liberated as meditation, but when there is no mindfulness it still has the perception of solidity. In your dreams, you are sometimes deluded and sometimes not. At this level, there is fixation on emptiness, with such thoughts as "All the phenomena of appearances and existences are nothing but emptiness" and so on.

MEDIUM NONELABORATION

You are purified of fixation on emptiness, on the reality of thoughts, and so on, though there remains the impurity of a subtle fixation on the reality of external appearances. During subsequent attainment and sleep, there may or may not be delusion and perception of solidity. In your practice, too, there can be many different levels and both progress and regress.

GREAT NONELABORATION

You completely cut through all conceptual embellishments concerning samsara and nirvana, outer appearances and the mind. You become liberated from attachment to whether there are appearances or no appearances, emptiness or no emptiness, and so on. During most of your waking hours you have continuous meditation, while in your dreams you are occasionally fixated on delusions. However, at this level there still isn't an uninterrupted, unchanging continuity of mindfulness. Therefore you still need some control of mindfulness.

In brief, the key point of the stage of nonelaboration is that it is principally the experience of emptiness and the experience of the unreality of everything. Therefore there is the possibility of a decline in devotion, pure perception, compassion, and so on. So it's important not to become overpowered by the obstacle of emptiness becoming your enemy.

At this level, seeing the essence of nonelaboration depends on becoming purified of the stain of certainty that is fixation on emptiness. Attaining mastery of it depends on becoming free from hope and fear concerning appearances and emptiness, and on cutting through conceptual embellishment of the path. Thoughts arising as meditation depend on training, during both subsequent appearances and sleep, in the realization of meditation that recognizes all movement of thought to be nothing other than emptiness. The arising of qualities depends on being connected with such apparent signs of accomplishment as the twelve hundred qualities from seeing the truth of the realized meaning. The full understanding of relative truth and planting the seed of the form kāyas depends on gaining certainty in the radiant power of emptiness manifesting as causes and results, and on then establishing the factors of dependent origination through bodhicitta and prayer. It's been taught that we must know these and other categories.

c. One-taste yoga

When you have fully realized the level of nonelaboration, you realize that all dualistic names and categories, such as samsara and nirvana, appearance and emptiness, generation and completion, relative and ultimate, and so on, are of one taste in the mahāmudrā. You are able to absorb all the path's Dharma teachings into self-knowing.

THE LESSER LEVEL OF ONE TASTE

This is while there is still some bondage to certainty or to fixation on experience.

MEDIUM ONE TASTE

This is when you are purified of fixation on experience and realize the inseparability of appearances and mind. The realizer's knowing and that which is realized are not fixated upon as having either a separate reality or a single one. Therefore there is liberation from subject and object.

GREATER ONE TASTE

This is when all phenomena appear as the "one taste of multiplicity" so that there is the increasing power of wisdom, which is the realization of one taste itself arising as multiplicity. The great holders of the practice lineage have taught that at this time meditation and post-meditation become blended.

All appearances and thoughts have the primordial nature of the dharmakāya, or the mahāmudrā, but there is a perception of solidity, a duality of subject and object, and so on, in relation to appearances, to illusion. If you train in self-knowing mindfulness of these things, they will be spontaneously liberated. This occurs in the lower yogas, too, but the training on this stage doesn't require a separate mindfulness or recognition, as any appearance or arising is itself enough. Seeing the essence of one taste depends on that. The mastery of it depends on the one taste arising as multiplicity and there not being any residue of subtle attachment to remedy. Thoughts arising as meditation depend on there being neither bondage nor liberation in the unrestricted appearance of all perceptions to the six consciousnesses. The arising of qualities depends on wisdom controlling all inner and outer phenomena and having the autonomy of performing miraculous emanations and transformations. Understanding the relative depends on the cause and result of power over appearances and existences being adopted as the path, which occurs through blending mind and appearances so that there is realization of the one taste as multiplicity. Planting the seed of the form kāyas depends on the treasury of benefiting others being opened by the power of effortless, all-pervading compassion.

d. Nonmeditation yoga

When you have completed the yoga of one taste, you will be purified of all dualistic appearances, such as meditation or no meditation, distraction or no distraction. All appearances will be liberated as the great primordial meditation.

LESSER NONMEDITATION

This is when, at night or at other times, there is a subtle fixation on the illusion-like nature of the propensities for subsequent appearances.

MEDIUM NONMEDITATION

This is when you are completely purified of fixation on illusion. Day and night, everything is one great meditation, and the true nature is manifest. However, you are still not free from wisdom's own obscuration, which is a subtle self-illuminating aspect of consciousness that is the "stain of knowledge."

GREATER NONMEDITATION

This is when there is the complete elimination of the subtle obscuration of knowledge, which is like the remainder of the ālaya consciousness and is the failure to recognize nonthought. The mother and child luminosity blend together, so that everything ripens as the single quintessence of the dharmakāya, the total expanse of wisdom. This is also called *true, complete buddhahood*. It is the final result.

It's taught that seeing the essence of nonmeditation depends on being purified of the "knowledge of experience," such as habituation to repeated meditation on the full realization of one taste. The mastery of nonmeditation depends on the wisdom of realization being free of all the subtlest stains of ignorance and all the propensities for objects of knowledge.

Thoughts arise as meditation through the ālaya's propensities dissolving into dharmadhātu wisdom. Qualities appear through the material body becoming a rainbow body, through the mind becoming the dharmakāya, through infinite pure realms appearing, or through liberation. The seeds of the form kāyas manifest through the body as a "wheel of inexhaustible adornments," effortlessly benefiting beings throughout space. All relative aspects are purified into the essential nature through all the great qualities of buddhahood being complete. Past Kagyüpas have explained these and all other very subtle categories.

2. A brief summary of the four yogas: [the way in which the four yogas arise in sequence]

One-pointedness is being able to remain in meditation for as long as you wish. Nonelaboration is the ordinary mind recognizing itself and the realization of baselessness and sourcelessness. One taste is when attachment to the dualism of samsara and nirvana is liberated within knowing. Nonmeditation is the purification of all stains, which are certainties and propensities.

In particular, during one-pointed yoga the difference between meditation and post-meditation is whether you are in stillness or not. During nonelaboration, the difference between meditation and post-meditation is whether you have mindfulness or not. In the one-taste yoga and above, meditation and post-meditation are inseparably blended.

Also, one-pointed yoga is when the nature of thoughts arises as nonthought. Nonelaboration is when they arise as emptiness. One taste is when they arise as equality. Nonmeditation is when they arise transcending the intellect.

Also, during one-pointedness, delusion arises just as it is. Within nonelaboration, it is realized to be baseless and sourceless. During one taste, delusion arises as wisdom. In nonmeditation, there are no longer the terms *delusion* and *no delusion*.

Also, each one has its own consummation: the supreme realization in one-pointedness is the inseparability of stillness and movement; in nonelaboration, it is the inseparability of delusion and liberation; in one taste, it is the inseparability of appearances and mind; in nonmeditation, it is the inseparability of meditation and post-meditation.

Also, in one-pointedness, the mind has the perception of solidity. In nonelaboration the mind has meditation and post-meditation. In one taste the mind has union. In nonmeditation the mind is manifest.

Also, during one-pointedness, thoughts are subjugated. During nonelaboration, thoughts are cut through. During one taste, self-arising wisdom appears from within. During nonmeditation that wisdom becomes stable.

To sum up, it seems the list of divisions and categories is endless and indescribable, but the most important thing we need to know and the only thing that matters is recognizing the true nature, the true meaning of the mind exactly as it is, and to know how to maintain the natural state of the ordinary mind, just as it happens to be, without polluting it with mental fabrication. According to Jñānaḍākinī Niguma:

> If you do not know that whatever appears is meditation,
> how can you attain it through relying on remedies?
> You cannot eliminate objects and conditions by eliminating them,
> but if you know they are illusions, they are spontaneously liberated.[185]

Most Dharma practitioners in these times are proud and bound tightly by this world's bondage. They are interested only in accumulating food, clothes, happiness, desires, objects, and artifacts for this life. Some have no control over their own minds because they're intoxicated by the poison that is their pride and arrogance of knowing many terms and teachings.

There are a few people interested in meditation on the definitive meaning, but lacking a genuine teacher and teachings, they are imprisoned in the discomfort of forced meditation. Not knowing how to practice open spaciousness, they practice a lot of stupid meditation, bought at the cost of their life force.

Most other meditators are bad; they're all talk, they're like an empty bellows or a stew made from lungs, and the mountains and valleys are filled with them. In such times as these, there's little point in teaching the qualities of the four yogas. It's like describing water in a desert.

The foremost worthy ones, those with unalloyed experience and realization, don't rely on external words and letters. Their wisdom is from meditation; it has come from within. So I'm well aware that there's no need for teachings such as mine that resemble someone describing some faraway place they've never seen.

Worthy individuals with diligence who rely on a pure teacher, receive blessing, and dedicate themselves to practice are genuine individuals who gain the realizations and experiences of the four yogas as taught here and elsewhere. They also incidentally pass through the entire five paths and ten levels of the common vehicles. It is said in the *King of Samādhis Sutra*:

> Whatever man holds this supreme samādhi,
> wherever that Dharma holder goes,
> [he will completely illuminate all beings]
> and will have a perfectly peaceful conduct and mind.
>
> He will also attain the ten levels:
> Perfect Joy, Stainless, Shining, Blazing,
> Difficult to Master, Manifest, Gone Far,
> Undisturbed, Excellent Intelligence, and Dharma Clouds.[186]

[3. A supplement that explains how the sutra tradition's paths and levels are completely included within the four yogas]

First, on the lesser, medium, and greater stages of the path of accumulation, there appear the four mindfulnesses, the four complete eliminations, and the four bases of miraculous powers. However, the way in which these are completely included within the swift path of mahāmudrā instructions is as follows:

First, there are the general preliminaries, in which there is the contemplation on the suffering of samsara, the difficulty of attaining the freedoms and wealths, the impermanence of life, and so on. This naturally includes:

   a. The mindfulness of the impurity of the body
   b. The mindfulness of the sensation of suffering
   c. The mindfulness of the impermanence of the mind
   d. The mindfulness of the selflessness of phenomena

Therefore, when you have experienced, contemplated, and gained certainty in the key points of [the general preliminaries], you will have traversed the lesser path of accumulation.

In the same way, taking refuge, developing bodhicitta, reciting the hundred syllables, and offering the mandala include the four complete eliminations:

   a. Not giving rise to bad actions
   b. Rejecting those that have arisen
   c. Developing good qualities
   d. Increasing those that have been developed

Therefore this is traversing the medium path of accumulation. Subsequently, the four bases of miraculous powers are in the guru yoga:

   a. One-pointed devotion to the guru is aspiration as a basis for miraculous powers.
   b. Prayer [to the guru] is diligence as a basis for miraculous powers.
   c. Receiving the four empowerments is conduct as a basis for miraculous powers.
   d. The final blending of the guru with your own mind is the mind's samādhi as a basis for miraculous powers.

This is traversing the greater path of accumulation.

The Perfection Vehicle teaches that through completing the path of accumulation you develop such qualities as being able to go to pure realms and see the faces of nirmāṇakāya buddhas. The mahāmudrā corresponds with that view, because the supreme guru is the essence of the three kāyas of buddhahood and all his "realms of pupils" are nothing other than nirmāṇakāya realms.

The stages of lesser, medium, and greater one-pointedness correspond to [the four levels of] the path of engagement:

a. Seeing the essence of the mind is *heat*.

b. Developing certainty in that is *summit*.

c. Being unaffected by circumstances is *patience*.

d. The continuous experience of one-pointedness is the path of engagement's worldly *supreme quality*.

During this stage, the specific qualities of the *five powers* arise:

a. The arising of limitless certainty is the power of faith.

b. Viewing the meaning without distraction is the power of mindfulness.

c. Not having laziness as an obstacle is the power of diligence.

d. An unbroken continuity of meditation is the power of samādhi.

e. The realization of the definitive meaning is the power of wisdom.

Each of those five develop into consummations of their power, which are called *strengths*. Therefore, when the three levels of one-pointedness are realized, you have completed the path of engagement.

At the level of nonelaboration, you enter the path of seeing the realized truth that you have learned about but have never seen before. This level naturally includes the meditations on the aspects of enlightenment taught in the Perfection Vehicle:

a. Remaining in the meaning of the true nature of phenomena, exactly as it is, is the enlightenment aspect of *samādhi*.
b. Being untainted by afflictions is the enlightenment aspect of the *perfect differentiation of phenomena*.
c. Mere mindfulness of samādhi spontaneously purifying stains on the path of seeing is the enlightenment aspect of *mindfulness*.
d. Freedom from the distraction of laziness is the enlightenment aspect of *diligence*.
e. The experience of immaculate joy is the enlightenment aspect of *joy*.
f. The purification of all faults is the enlightenment aspect of *total purification*.
g. The realization of the equality of samsara and nirvana is the enlightenment aspect of *equality*.

Thus all the seven aspects [of enlightenment] are completed. Moreover, you attain the many qualities and countless samādhis of the path of seeing. Some teach that you attain both the first level [of enlightenment] (*bhūmi*) and the path of meditation on perfecting the three [levels of] nonelaboration and reaching one taste. However, most others teach that you reach the first level [of enlightenment] on seeing the nature of nonelaboration and developing the path of seeing. Clearly there is no definitive conclusion concerning this because beings have different capabilities. There must certainly be varying natures and speeds of progressing through the paths.

When you have developed the true realization of the path of seeing, you will have created the source or foundation for all qualities. That is why it's said that you have attained a level [of enlightenment]. From the *Avataṃsaka Sutra*:

> On attaining the level they become free from five fears—
> of having no livelihood, of death, of not being praised,

of the lower existences, and of assemblies—and so are free of anxiety.[187]

Thus the qualities become greater and greater within the ten levels. When you reach the levels, this is called the *path of meditation*, because you are familiarizing yourself with the meaning of the path of seeing. On this level you practice the eight aspects of the noble path. All meditation is nothing but immaculate samādhi, but during post-meditation you are polluted and familiarizing yourself with the noble eightfold path. These eight are: correct view, correct realization, correct speech, correct action, correct livelihood, correct effort, correct mindfulness, and correct samādhi.

In brief, these accomplishments have the quality of being purely unmistaken. Therefore they truly have the many distinguishing qualities of the superior actions in the lower vehicles.

THE FIRST LEVEL [OF ENLIGHTENMENT]

The first level is called Perfect Joy because there is supreme joy at these special qualities. During this stage, "meditation sessions" are a birthless state without thought and in "subsequent [attainment]," through [seeing phenomena] as being like illusions, you benefit beings primarily by accomplishing the perfection of generosity through giving away, without fear or sadness, your head, limbs, and so on. You continue traversing the path in this way, passing through the sequence of the ten perfections combined with the ten levels. This is what is taught in extensive detail within the general vehicles. In this teaching, however:

a. The first level is called Perfect Joy, because the joy of samādhi greatly increases during the first level of nonelaboration.

b. The second level is called Stainless, because of freedom from all the stains of meditation.

c. The third level is called Shining, because of benefiting beings through the power of the realized meaning.

d. The fourth level is called Brilliance, because of the increase in revealing buddhahood's qualities of greatness during the medium level of nonelaboration.

e. The fifth level is called Difficult to Conquer, because of realizing the union of emptiness and compassion, which purifies all the stains of propensities, which are so difficult to purify.

f. The sixth level is called Manifest, because it is reached through the great level of nonelaboration becoming manifest. This is the realization that samsara and nirvana are birthless.

The śrāvakas and pratyekabuddhas can reach those first six levels also.

g. The seventh level is called Gone Far, because at the beginning level of one taste, such dualistic appearances as meditation and post-meditation, samsara and nirvana, and so on are liberated in union.

h. The eighth level is called Unwavering because at the medium level of one taste, there is no deviation from the true mindfulness that is the quality of realization.

i. The ninth level is called Excellent Intelligence because at the great level of one taste, all stains apart from subtle illusion-like dualistic appearances are purified.

j. The tenth level is generally known as Dharma Clouds, which in this teaching is the lesser and medium levels of nonmeditation. This is when even the subtlest dualistic appearances are spontaneously purified and you fully attain the qualities of the paths and levels. Nevertheless, there still remains the very subtlest obscuration of knowledge, which is the propensity for fixation—the remaining stain on the ālaya consciousness. At this level, you will have the same qualities as bodhisattvas who are lords of the tenth level.

The true state of buddhahood is when you reach the conclusion of the supreme, ultimate path of the common vehicles. This is when the stain of not recognizing nonthought, which is the subtle propensity of the knowledge obscuration, dissolves into the nature of vajra-like wisdom, which is the great self-arising self-knowing. You are then eternally freed from every obscuration; you have completely perfected the wisdom that knows the ultimate nature and the wisdom that knows relative multiplicity; and you have perfected wisdom, compassion, and power.

In the context of mahāmudrā, this is called *great nonmeditation*. In the general Mantrayāna, this is the eleventh level, Complete Illumination, and the twelfth level, Attachment-Free Lotus. At these levels there are no obscurations of karma, afflictions, and propensities, and there is no actual traversing of a path of purification, but their names indicate the distinguishing aspects or special characteristics of an increase in qualities. Both these special, internal levels manifest in a single instant.

The final level of buddhahood is called the thirteenth, or [the state of] the sixth [buddha], Vajradhara. This has benefit for oneself, which is the complete attainment of the dharmakāya, and benefit for others, which is its power of manifestation as form kāyas that continuously bring great benefit to all beings throughout space until samsara is emptied.

Progressing through the [first four] paths and the [ten] levels is called the *path of training*. When you reach their conclusion and there is nowhere higher to go, that is called the *path of no training*. For the Mantrayāna, the ultimate result is the thirteenth, or [the level of] Vajradhara.

What qualities do you gain when you reach the levels?

1. On attaining the first level:
   - You can go simultaneously to a hundred nirmāṇakāya realms in the ten directions.
   - You can see a hundred buddhas and hear their teachings.
   - You can perform simultaneously a hundred different acts

of generosity, such as giving away, without regret, your body, life, possessions, kingdom, child, wife, and so on.

- You can radiate simultaneously a hundred different kinds of light rays, such as radiating a red light and reabsorbing it as white light, radiating a yellow light and reabsorbing it as blue light, radiating many light rays and reabsorbing them as few light rays, and so on.

- You can teach simultaneously a hundred entranceways into the Dharma to accord with the nature and thoughts of a hundred different individual pupils.

- You can rest simultaneously in a hundred different kinds of samādhis that have been taught in the *Mother of the Conquerors*,[188] such as the "heroic," "massed forces," "awesome lion," and so on.

- You can manifest simultaneously a hundred different miracles: You can fly up into the sky, sink down into the earth, pass unimpeded through mountains and rocks, stand on water, blaze with flames from your upper body while water gushes from your lower half, do those one after the other, transform one thing into many or many things into one, and so on.

You become thus endowed with these seven qualities each in a hundredfold form. In the same way, sequentially:

2. On the second level, there is a thousandfold form of each of these seven.

3. [On the third level, there is a ten-thousandfold form of each of these seven.][189]

4. On the fourth level, there is a hundred-thousandfold form of each of these seven.

5. On the fifth level, there is a millionfold form of each of these seven.

6. On the sixth level, there is a ten-millionfold form of each of these seven.

7. On the seventh level, there is a hundred-millionfold form of each of these seven.

8. On the eighth level, there is a billionfold form of each of these seven.

9. On the ninth level, there is a ten-billionfold form of each of these seven.

10. On the tenth level, there is a trillionfold form of each of these seven.

11. On the eleventh level, there is a ten-trillionfold form of each of these seven.

12. On the twelfth level, there is a hundred-trillionfold form of each of these seven.

13. On the thirteenth level, the manifest nature of the three kāyas of buddhahood, or Vajradhara, has an infinite form of each of these qualities. They are incalculable because their nature is beyond the scope of the intellect.

Thus all ten levels and five paths taught in the common vehicles are perfectly complete and distinct within the mahāmudrā, the pinnacle of all the vehicles. Naturally, someone who truly manifests the four yogas will gradually—or immediately—complete every quality of the paths and levels. However, it is a special quality of the secret, swift Mantrayāna path that some don't reveal these qualities as actually perceivable characteristics on the apparent level. For example, most beings, such as birds and wild beasts, are born from their mothers' wombs and don't become fully developed for a while. The gradualists are like that. However, the garuda, who is the lord of birds, and the lion, who is the king of wild beasts, already have their complete powers inside the egg or mother's womb. At that time they can't be seen, but as soon as they're born, their three powers[190] are fully developed so that they can accomplish all activities, such as flying in the sky with their mother. In the same way, some yogins do not have actually visible signs while they are still confined within their material bodies, but on being freed from the traps that are their bodies, the result simultaneously ripens as the fully developed power of their qualities. There are also numerous individuals who, having accomplished the path that unites method and wisdom, visibly manifest the signs of that path, such as miraculous powers and clairvoyance, in that very life.

Basically you attain freedom in the wisdom that knows the equality of space and wisdom, the intellect-transcending true nature, and the intrinsic nature of the mind itself. Otherwise all you will get is just a few signs of heat through the practice of the generation and completion, the channels, winds, drops, and so on. In these times there are so many siddhas possessed by the *gongpo* demons who rejoice in these few signs, prize them, fixate on them as wonderful, become conceited, and herd themselves and others into the lower existences. Therefore I beseech those with critical minds to realize this for themselves.

That was a brief teaching on the view, meditation, and stages of the path. I now give a short teaching on the ancillary subject of how to enhance results through performing the conduct of "bringing into the path."

In general, most Mantrayāna paths have different kinds of conduct, such as the three categories of elaborate, simple, and very simple conduct. There are also many different categories such as secret conduct, public conduct, *vidyāvrata*, and victorious conduct. Most of these are primarily for enhancing the results of generation- and completion-stage practices. Here the only conduct that is highly valued is the "completely excellent conduct," which maintains an intrinsic, intellect-transcending approach.

Even at the beginning, those who practice the preliminaries— gathering accumulations, purifying obscurations, and receiving blessings—should dedicate themselves to the completely excellent conduct: a behavior that is unpolluted by any stain from life's activities or from the eight worldly concerns, and gives no reason to feel ashamed.

In the middle stage, those engaged in the main practices—thoroughly examining view and meditation and gaining certainty in self-knowing—should dedicate themselves to the completely excellent conduct: beating out from within the nails of many thoughts; cutting through the mind's bondage of arrogant conceptual embellishments; mastering everything through knowing one thing; and becoming liberated from all through knowing one thing.[191]

In the end, there is the particular conduct to enhance the results of practice, for which there are different texts and practice instructions, but the essential point is to develop:

1. The conduct of a wounded deer, which means completely cutting through bondage to this world and wandering in uninhabited mountains.
2. The conduct that is like a lion running alongside ravines, which is not fearing negative circumstances.
3. The conduct that is like wind moving through the air, which is having no attachment to sensory pleasures.
4. The conduct like that of a lunatic, which means not involving yourself in either ending or engendering the eight worldly concerns.
5. The conduct that is like a spear being whirled in the air, which is allowing the mind to move freely as it wishes, unrestricted by the bondage of dualism.
6. The supreme, completely excellent conduct, which is cutting through the bondage of delusion, distraction, hope, and fear, and focusing solely on maintaining an unfabricated state, because even a hair tip of hidden, internal desire for signs, omens, experiences, realizations, siddhis, and so on, will only obscure the face of the ultimate nature, the dharmakāya.

Even if there are thoughts, afflictions, suffering, fear, pain, death, or anything that seems to be a special circumstance, don't hope for or depend on any remedial method other than knowing this main practice, the mahāmudrā, the ultimate nature. This is the king of all enhancement practices. Yogins who can practice it in this way gain power over all appearances and existences in samsara and nirvana; they are free from all obstacles; they accumulate an ocean of siddhis; the darkness of the two obscurations disappear; the sun of the signs of accomplishment rises; they find buddhahood in their own minds; and they open a treasury of benefit for beings. That is the nature [of this conduct].

But it's sad to now see meditators doing nothing but spending their lives planning, like a child by a pond of lotuses, thinking, "I'm going to choose this—no, that one would be better!" while having thrown away this all-sufficing jewel they had in their hands.

That concludes my brief teaching on the nature of the basis, the path, the view, and the meditation.

III. *The result mahāmudrā*

I will conclude with a brief teaching on the result mahāmudrā, which is the inseparability of the three kāyas, or the union of the two kāyas.

Yogins who see the face of the true nature, the basis mahāmudrā, have truly accomplished through their practice the mahāmudrā of view, meditation, and path. This is the manifestation of mahāmudrā as the final result, the ultimate truth, and the dharmakāya.

The essence of the dharmakāya is self-knowing. It is the original, unaltered wisdom, which is changeless, neither increases nor diminishes, primordially pervades all beings in the three realms, and manifests through the profound key methods of practice. There is no buddha or dharmakāya other than this. It is not something previously nonexistent that is newly created.

CHARACTERISTICS OF THE RESULT MAHĀMUDRĀ

It is called *possession of two wisdoms* because it has the wisdom that knows ultimate nature and the wisdom that knows relative multiplicity. It is called *possession of two purities* because its essence is primordially pure and it has also been purified of nonintrinsic connate stains. Therefore it is free from every stain that prevents seeing or knowing all the phenomena that can be known, and it has completely perfected every positive quality.

The dharmakāya's radiance, or wisdom's unimpeded display, is the manifestation of the saṃbhogakāya and nirmāṇakāya. These three kāyas have the qualities of the *seven aspects of union*. What are these seven? The three particular qualities of the saṃbhogakāya (enjoyment body):

1. The aspect of enjoyment, which is the continuous, eternal enjoyment of the profound and vast Mantrayāna Dharma wheel for the bodhisattvas in Akaniṣṭha.

2. The aspect of sexual union, which is union with a consort formed from light as a wisdom body with all the primary and secondary signs.

3. The aspect of great bliss, which is an uninterrupted continuity of great, immaculate bliss.

The three particular qualities of the nirmāṇakāya:

4. The aspect of being completely filled with compassion that is objectless compassion, which, like space, pervades everywhere.

5. The aspect of uninterrupted continuity, which is a vast, nonconceptual, naturally present activity that extends to the limits of samsara.

6. The aspect of noncessation, which is not to rest in the extreme of nirvana's peace.

The Mind of Mahāmudrā

The particular quality of the dharmakāya:
  7. The aspect of having no nature: this is the union of emptiness and compassion, transcending all conceptual elaboration.

One also guides with *eight qualities of lordship*:
  1. Lordship over body: having any form of any body in order to train particular beings
  2. Lordship over speech: the continuous turning of whatever Dharma wheel is necessary to train [particular beings]
  3. Lordship over mind: having nonconceptual compassion
  4. Lordship over miracles: having unimpeded, miraculous powers
  5. Lordship over omnipresence: having the true enlightenment of one taste, which is the equality of the three times, samsara and nirvana
  6. Lordship over desire: being unstained by desire, even if as many goddesses as there are atoms in twelve Mount Merus made offerings of sensory pleasures
  7. Lordship over the creation of whatever is desired: being able, like a wish-fulfilling jewel, to fulfill the hopes and desires of beings
  8. Lordship over residence: eternally dwelling in Akaniṣṭha dharmadhātu as the Dharma king of the three realms

"Guiding with the eight lordships" is primarily a synonym for the qualities of the saṃbhogakāya. The dharmakāya and saṃbhoga-kāya manifest the nirmāṇakāya as emanation-teachers who are like reflections of the moon in all the countless water bowls that are their pupils. The nirmāṇakāya is the appearance of infinite emanations in whatever form is necessary to teach beings, such as created, born, and great-enlightenment emanations.[192] They are called the "secret body, speech, and mind of the buddhas as a wheel of unceasing adornments."

THE CAUSE FOR THE KĀYAS TO ARISE

The dharmakāya is the result of truly accomplishing the ultimate—emptiness and mahāmudrā—while upon the path. The nirmāṇakāya is an aspect of it, or part of its method, because it arises through having developed pure bodhicitta, aspiration prayers, and so on. The saṃbhogakāya arises from the causes and results of meditation on the profound generation stage. The everlasting domain of the three kāyas' inseparability is the result not of doing those practices separately or alternately but of engaging in the union of method and wisdom, in the great complete purity from the triple aspects of conceptualization.

There are many more categories of these three kāyas and also of four, five, or more kāyas, which are essentially one but given different names in terms of aspects of qualities and activities. However, they are nothing other than the nature, radiance, and power of the present mind, which we call the three kāyas at the time of the result.

In the causal vehicles, the lower tantras, and so on, there are various traditions of explanation based on certain scriptures that were intended for particular circumstances or in which the true meaning is only implied. There appears to be controversy over these grounds for debate involving a lot of proofs and refutations. The disagreement is over whether the dharmakāya has a face and arms or not, whether it truly manifests a realm or not, whether buddhas have wisdom in their own individual beings or not, whether the two form kāyas have individual experiences of sensory perceptions or not, and so on. Each viewpoint may be valid in its own context, but in this quintessential essence of the vehicles, we don't depend on finding proofs for views in the lower vehicles. We have the viewpoint described as "in agreement with all and distinct from all."

What is this viewpoint? It has no attachment to such things as reality or unreality, existence or nonexistence, identity or nonidentity, arising or ceasing, coming or going, eternality or nothingness, to any phenomena within appearance or existence, within samsara or nirvana. Therefore it neither proposes, refutes, nor proves. Why? Because if we say that there is nonexistence, we fall into the extreme of nihilism, but if we say there is existence, we fall into the extreme of eternalism, and if we hold the belief that there is neither existence nor nonexistence, we are failing to transcend a state of mental fabrication.

As for others, if they say their perceptions exist, we can agree with that, because, through the infallibility of dependent origination and causes and results, there is an unceasing, unstoppable manifestation of appearances. If they say they have no existence, we can agree with that, because having no existing nature of their own whatsoever, appearances are never apart from emptiness. If they say that appearances are neither existent nor nonexistent, we can agree with that, too, because this does not fall into an extreme and is without partiality or bias.

In the deluded perceptions that arise from the propensities of impure beings, everything that appears as an external world and its inhabitants appears to be formed from the solid, material five elements. In the perception of yogins on the path, they are the unimpeded appearances of their own mind. For buddhas and bodhisattvas, it is the realm of self-illuminating wisdom. Thus, ultimately, everything is simply the display of the mind itself.

Similarly, for impure, deluded beings, their minds, and the mental events that are their thoughts, have the nature of karma, afflictions, and propensities. For yogins on the path, they are particular aspects of view, meditation, experience, and realization. For the buddhas, the three kāyas of the sugatas, they are the display of knowledge, compassion, and wisdom. Therefore, in the true nature of the basis, or cause, there isn't even an atom of difference, the only difference being whether one is thickly obscured by "imaginary" extrinsic obscurations, only partially obscured, or entirely free from obscuration.[193] The single key point is to relax in your own unaltered mind, the mahāmudrā, which is the essential meaning of never having been apart from, not being apart from, and never going to be apart from the union of the two kāyas, or the inseparability of the three kāyas, which is the essence of the basis, path, and result.

Those with composite intellects, who embellish or denigrate the noncomposite Dharma and who are attached to the extreme of words and to disputes between different traditions, are like childish people arguing about how far space extends. If you rest in a state of great, all-pervasive equality within unfabricated relaxation, you will no doubt be liberated in a state that transcends concepts of traveler and destination: the expanse of the naturally present result of the four yogas, the ten levels, the five paths, and the three kāyas.

Kye ho!

All beings, from mites upward,
are obscured by ignorance but are never apart from
the element of buddha nature, primordial innate liberation,
and the three kāyas of naturally present buddhahood.

The Buddha taught as many Dharma entranceways as there are
    pupils to be taught,
and yet they remain deluded by their own appearances,
in the bondage of wrong, mistaken, or erroneous paths.[194]
Those who travel the true, excellent path are [as rare as] fig
    flowers.[195]

Although the extremes do not exist, beings are chained by
    their belief in the extremes.
They do not know what it is they possess, like a poor woman
    who has a treasure.
They pollute with contrivance that which is uncontrived and
    self-arisen.

Without knowing how it is complete within them, what can
    they ever find?[196]

The merit of those with power and wealth falls under the
    power of the māras.
All who are arrogant through learning have minds like stiff-
    ened leather.[197]
Those who practice stupid, forced meditation strive to squeeze
    oil out of sand.
Who is there who will sit in the presence of the true nature, of
    the mahāmudrā?[198]

Alas! This supreme teaching that unites the sutras and tantras,
    the sun and the moon,
descends to the water goddess, with the vermilion clouds of a
    session's end.[199]
Why are you not saddened by having only its branches, and
    why, for the sake of this world's appearances,
do you deliberately throw your freedoms and wealths into the
    dust?

Oh, don't you see that the teaching of the practice lineage
is to look at your own natural face, the supreme, eternal goal,
while perfectly living on whatever food
you happen to obtain to sustain you in uninhabited mountains?

In such a time as this, when practitioners do not truly practice,
and actions that destroy the teachings are called the "meaning
    of the teachings,"
who could need, and who would want to read,
a book like this written by someone like me?

Texts written in black ink that even the author doesn't need
and are not respected by others can fill caves,

but if they're unable to tame even a few minds,
all the paper and ink does is tire out fingers.

For a long time someone has been insistently entreating me to
    write this,
and so as not to refuse to give him what he has asked for,
out of necessity, I've written whatever came to my mind,
so its words will be neither meaningful nor faultless.

What I have written is completely devoid of such things as
the discernment that is skillful in the medium of writing
or the experience of understanding this great subject matter;
so what else can it be but a cause for hilarity among scholars
    and siddhas?

Nevertheless, I have written this so as not to prevent the faint
    possibility
that a beautiful garland of jasmine flowers, blossoming
in the light of good aspiration, undarkened by bad motivation,
might adorn the ears of a few novice meditators like myself.

Through the power of the merit of writing this,
united with all stained and stainless merit in the three paths,
within samsara and nirvana, may the teachings of the practice
    lineage spread in all directions,
and may all beings manifest the result of mahāmudrā.

The vidyādhara of Mengom, Tsultrim Sangpo,[200] asked me
repeatedly over a long time to write an extensive and detailed
text for practitioners of mahāmudrā to understand the enhancement and the signs on the path's stages. However, I felt there
was no need for such a text as there were already countless deep
and profound teachings within the collected works of the past
Kagyü masters.

In particular, there are the profound mahāmudrā [instructions] that kind refuge lords have bestowed upon me out of their compassion: such renowned Sarma teachings as the *Innate Union,*[201] the *four letters,*[202] the *Ganges,*[203] the *Letterless,*[204] the *root symbols,*[205] the *essence of practice* teachings,[206] the *inconceivable secret,*[207] the *illumination of wisdom,*[208] the *fivefold,*[209] the *wish-fulfilling jewel,*[210] the *six nails of essential meaning,*[211] and many practice instructions.

I also received through their kindness such Nyingma mahāmudrā teachings as: the *Vast Expanse Free from Extremes*; the *Sun's Essence*; *Giving Rise to the Single Knowing*; *Dispelling the Darkness of Ignorance*; *Seeing the Naked Intrinsic Nature*;[212] and also many [mahāmudrā teachings] from the termas.

However, being carried away by waves of karma, afflictions, and distraction, I was unable to develop even the tiniest fraction of experience and realization. Therefore I didn't have the confidence to write this text. Nevertheless, I have now written this blindly in the dark so as not to leave the request unfulfilled. I pray from my heart that I will not bring shame to the wise scholars and siddhas.

May the merit of this cause all my old mothers—all beings throughout space—to attain the sublime state of unsurpassable enlightenment within their lifetime.

Maṅgalaṃ bhavantu
(May they have good fortune!)

A lazy man, who is not Götsangpa but is known as Götsangpa, wrote this in Palri Götsang cave, which is not Latö Götsang.[213]

May there be goodness! May there be goodness! May there be goodness!

Notes

1 Other important Kagyü texts on mahāmudrā are available in translation. There are two texts by the Ninth Karmapa Wangchuk Dorjé: *Mahāmudra: The Ocean of Definitive Meaning*, trans. Elizabeth Callahan (Seattle: Nitartha, 2001), and *The Mahāmudrā: Eliminating the Darkness of Ignorance*, trans. Alexander Berzin (Dharamsala: Library of Tibetan Works and Archives, 1978). There are also two texts by Dakpo Tashi Namgyal: *Mahāmudrā: The Moonlight—Quintessence of Mind and Meditation*, trans. Lobsang Lhalungpa (Boston: Wisdom, 2006), and *Clarifying the Natural State: A Principal Guidance Manual for Mahamudra*, trans. Erik Pema Kunsang (Hong Kong: Rangjung Yeshe, 2001). See also Daniel P. Brown, *Pointing Out the Great Way: The Stages of Meditation in the Mahāmudrā Tradition* (Boston: Wisdom, 2006).

2 Peter Alan Roberts, *Mahāmudrā and Related Instructions: Core Teachings of the Kagyü School* (Boston: Wisdom, 2011). The longer volume also included a compilation of lectures on general subjects by Gampopa; Sherap Jungné's *Single Viewpoint* and three supplements that codify the viewpoints of Jikten Sumgön, the founder of the Drigung Kagyü; a text on the six Dharmas of Nāropa by the Sixth Shamarpa Chökyi Wangchuk; an extensive guide to the various aspects and levels of tantra by Dakpo Tashi Namgyal; and an extensive commentary by the Eighth Situ Rinpoché on the Third Karmapa's *Prayer for the Definitive Meaning, the Mahāmudrā*.

3 For a detailed description of both stages, see Jamgön Kongtrul, *Creation and Completion: Essential Points of Tantric Meditation*, trans. Sarah Harding (Boston: Wisdom, 1996).

4 For further reading on the generation or completion stages, see Jamgön Kongtrul Lodrö Tayé, *The Treasury of Knowledge, book 8, part 3: The Elements of Tantric Practice* (Ithaca, NY: Snow Lion, 2008), and *book 8, part 4: Esoteric Instructions* (Ithaca, NY: Snow Lion, 2007). Also, Daniel Cozort, *Highest Yoga Tantra* (Ithaca, NY: Snow Lion, 1986).

5 For further information on this topic, see Shamarpa Chokyi Wangchuk, "The Quintesence of Nectar," in Roberts, *Mahāmudrā and Related Instructions*, 333–72. Also, Jamgön Kongtrul Lodrö Tayé, *The Treasury of Knowledge, book 8, part 3*, 123–216, and *book 8, part 4*, 149–208. Also, Glen H. Mullin, *The Practice of the Six Yogas of Naropa* (Ithaca, NY: Snow Lion, 1997); Lama Thubten Yeshe, *The Bliss of Inner Fire: Heart Practice of the Six Yogas of Naropa* (Boston: Wisdom, 1998); Garma C. C. Chang, *The Six Yogas of Naropa and Teachings on Mahamudra* (Ithaca, NY: Snow Lion, 1986). Also, W. Y. Evans-Wentz, ed., *Tibetan Yoga and Secret Doctrines* (London: Oxford University Press, 1935).

6 See, for instance, the yoga tantras introduced into Tibet in the eighth century, where it means the completely visualized deity.

7 For an in-depth study of Saraha, see Kurtis R. Schaeffer, *Dreaming the Great Brahmin: Tibetan Traditions of the Buddhist Poet-Saint Saraha* (Oxford: Oxford University Press, 2004).

8 The dates in *The Blue Annals* do not specify the year elements, and in his translation, Roerich chose 1007/10–87, dates that have commonly been repeated. Those dates, however, do not correspond with the biographies of Maitripa's pupils. It seems clear that he had to have passed away before Vajrapāṇi moved to Nepal in 1066.

9 For further information on Nāropa see [Lhatsun Rinchen Namgyal], *Life and Teaching of Naropa*, trans. Herbert V. Guenther (Boston: Shambhala, 1986).

10 Ronald M. Davidson, *Indian Esoteric Buddhism* (New York: Columbia University Press, 2003), 317.

11 Tailikapāda (Tilopa), *Mahāmudrā Instructions*.

12 Gö Lotsāwa, *The Blue Annals*, trans. George N. Roerich (Calcutta: Motilal Banarsidass, 1949), 844.

13 The dates for Marpa's life vary in different biographies. For example, Kathok Tsewang Norbu lists ten variant dates for Marpa's life that are found in Kagyü histories, which in Western years would be: b. 991, 997–1084, 1000–1081/85/88, 1002–81, 1006–94/96, 1011–96, 1012–93, 1012–97, 1021–1109, 1024–1107 (*Clear Brief Correct Account of a Definite Chronology*, Kathok Rikzin Tsewang Norbu's Collected Works, vol. 3, 640). His life story is primarily known through the nonhistorical but compelling work of Tsangnyön Heruka: *The Life of Marpa the Translator: Seeing All Accomplishes All*, trans. Nalanda Translation Committee (Boston: Shambhala, 1982). See also, Cécile Ducher, *Building Tradition: The Lives of Mar-pa the Translator* (Munich: Indus Verlag, 2014).

14 Gö Lotsāwa, *Blue Annals*, 843.

15 Ibid.

16 Ibid.

17 *Amanasi skor nyer drug*, the collective name for twenty-four texts by Maitripa and two by his pupils. Toh 2229–54 Tengyur, rgyud, *wi*, 104b7–177a7.

18 Gö Lotsāwa, *Blue Annals*, 844–47.

19 Examples of alternative dates: Kathok Tsewang Norbu settles on 1028–1111 in his *Clear Brief Correct Account of Definite Chronology*; it is 1048–1129 in Dorjé Dzeö's *Precious Treasury that Is the Source of All that Is Required*; Gyalthangpa gives 1055–1128 in his *Golden Succession of the Kagyü*; and the anonymous *Biography and Songs of Shepai Dorjé* has 1036–1123.

20 Tsangnyön Heruka, *The Life of Milarepa*, trans. Andrew Quintman (New York: Penguin, 2010); *The Hundred Thousand Songs of Milarepa*, trans. Garma C. C. Chang (Boston: Shambhala, 1989).

21 For further information on Tsangnyön Heruka, see Stefan Larsson, *Crazy for Wisdom* (Leiden: Brill, 2012). Also, Andrew Quintman, *The Yogin and the Madman* (New York: Columbia University Press, 2014).

22 Tsangnyön, *The Life of Marpa t*

23 For further information on Rechungpa, see Peter Alan Roberts, *The Biographies of Rechungpa* (Abingdon, Oxon: Routledge, 2007).

24 For further information on Gampopa see Jampa Mackenzie Stewart, *The Life of Gampopa* (Ithaca, NY: Snow Lion, 1995).

25 Peter Alan Roberts, "The Evolution of the Biographies of Milarepa and Rechungpa," in *Lives Lived, Lives Imagined*, 181–203 (Boston: Wisdom, 2010).

26 *Thar pa rin po che'i rgyan.* This text, already available in several English-language translations as the *Jewel Ornament of Liberation*, will appear in a translation by Ken Holmes in volume 10 of *The Library of Tibetan Classics*, the volume on the stages of the doctrine (*bstan rim*) genre.

27 Tatsak Tsewang Gyal, *Dharma History from Lhorong* (pp. 177–80), has earth bird to iron ox (1129–81); Gö Lotsāwa, *Blue Annals* (pp. 463–65), has fire monkey to earth ox (1116–69).

28 Gö Lotsāwa, *Blue Annals*, 463.

29 For more information on this subject, see Karma Thinley, *The History of the Sixteen Karmapas of Tibet* (Boulder, CO: Prajna Press, 1980).

30 Also called Marpa (*smar pa*) Kagyü, not to be confused with Marpa (*mar pa*) Kagyü, the name for all Kagyü lineages. Gangri Karma Rinpoche, the present Martsang Kagyü lineage holder, is working to reestablish it as an independent school.

31 The Nedo Kagyü teachings are also an essential part of the Palyul Nyingma school, which arose in eastern Tibet in the seventeenth century based on the termas of Namchö Mingyur Dorjé (1645–67). Penor Rinpoche (1932–2009), the late head of the Nyingma school, was also the Palyul Nyingma throneholder.

32 Lharipa Namkha Ö, a direct pupil of Lama Shang and Shönu Lha's own teacher.

33 This is a reference to Gampopa, also known as Dakpo Lhajé or Dakpo Rinpoché.

34 Aśvaghoṣa, *A Letter of Consolation* (*Śokavinodana*), 33a6.

35 Ibid., 2:59, 6a6.

36 *Bhadrakarātrisūtra*, 162b2.

37 *Aphorisms* (*Udānavarga*), 1:33, 209b2. Shönu Lha either paraphrased this passage or was using a different translation.

38 Aśvaghoṣa, *A Letter of Consolation* (*Śokavinodana*), 33b3.

39 *Entering the Conduct of a Bodhisattva (Bodhicaryāvatāra)*, 6:59, 16b7.

40 Ibid., 2:41–42, 5b2.

41 *Mahāyāna Uttaratantraśāstra.* The quotation is not to be found in this text. It may be intended as a summation rather than a quote of 4:50, 69b5: "There are five pathways of beings in the beginningless birth and death of samsara. Just as ordure has no pleasant smell, the five kinds of beings have no happiness. Their constant suffering is like that in contact with fire, weapons, lye, and so on." However, the quote here is given in verse, and these lines are not to be found either in the Kangyur or Tengyur.

42 Śāntideva, *Bodhicaryāvatāra*, 4:20, 8b6.

43 Ibid., 1:4, 1b5.

44 *Sangs rgyas chos dang...* This is presumably the ubiquitous prayer:

> In the Buddha, the Dharma, and the supreme Sangha
> I take refuge until enlightenment;
> through the merit of my deeds such as generosity,
> may I achieve enlightenment for the benefit of beings.

45 The mantra first appears as one of three variants in the *Compendium of Truths (Tattvasaṃgraha)*, 34a7.

46 In which the eating of food is transformed into an offering practice.

47 Vajradhara is called the sixth Buddha because he is in addition to the higher tantra system of five buddha families with their principal buddhas: Vairocana, Akṣobhya, Ratnasambhava, Amitābha, and Amoghasiddhi. As the embodiment of the dharmakāya, he is also considered the source from which these five buddhas emanate.

48 The Tibetan definition is anything of a precious appearance found in rivers, as it is believed the action of the water has brought out the essence of the stones. The Sanskrit word has been identified as various gems, but one Sanskrit verse has "*aśmagarbha* jewels among rubies like green parrots among red foliage," implying an emerald, which is also called *marakata* (Tib. *mar gad*).

49 *Enlightenment of Vairocana (Mahāvairocanābhisambodhi)*, 169a1.

50 *Atyayajñānasūtra*, 153a.

51 Mikyö Dorjé's commentary on *Entering the Middle Way* attributes the quote to Lama Shang (150b6) but does not specify the source. It also includes a second line between these two, "develop the aspiration to benefit beings."

52 Ibid., 150b6.

53 Source unidentified.

54 *Eight-Thousand-Verse Perfection of Wisdom Sutra* (*Aṣṭasāhasri-kāprajñāpāramitā*), 3a3. The citation in this edition varies slightly from the canonical version, which begins: "Thus that mind is not mind..."

55 Source unidentified.

56 Saraha, *Dohakoṣagīti*, 72b4.

57 "Autumn's cloudless sky" refers to the season after the monsoon, when the rains have cleared the air of dust and the clouds have vanished.

58 Dampa Sangyé, per Kunga Rinchen's *Opening the Eyes*, 47a5.

59 Source unidentified.

60 Dampa Sangyé, per Kunga Rinchen's *Opening the Eyes*, 45a3.

61 *Sdom pa rgya mtsho'i rgyud*. This text has not been identified.

62 Source unidentified.

63 *Jñānaguhyadīparatnopadeśatantra*, 4a1.

64 Yeshé Jungné, *The Methods for Entering the Mahāyāna Yoga*, 11b5.

65 Gampopa (1079–1153), a.k.a. Dakpo Lhajé, considered to be the rebirth of Kumāra ("the youth") Candraprabha from the *King of Samādhis Sutra*.

66 The site of Gampopa's monastery, the first Kagyü monastery, founded in 1137, when Gampopa was around fifty-eight years old. The text has the variant form Daklha Gompo (*dwags lha sgom po*).

67 Lama Shang.

68 The two Buddha statues are those said to have been brought to Tibet by two queens of King Songtsen Gampo in the seventh century. That of the Chinese queen is in the Jokhang, Lhasa's principal temple, and that brought by the Nepalese queen is in the Ramoché temple in Lhasa.

69 There is an annotation to the original Tibetan text identifying the lama as Lharipa Namkha Ö, even though the text reads as if it is

Lama Shang himself. "The emanation of Shang" could be interpreted both ways. Namkha Ö, however, was a direct pupil of Lama Shang, of Düsum Khyenpa (who founded the Karma Kagyü), and particularly of Taklung Thangpa (who founded the Taklung Kagyü).

70 *Spang gshong lha ri*, "pasture-basin divine mountain," the location of Shönu Lha's monastery.

71 Sanskrit for Lha Shönu, "young deity."

72 Tatsak Tsewang Gyal, *Dharma History*, 181–99; Gö Lotsāwa, *Blue Annals*, 711–15. Also known as Shang Rinpoché and Yudrakpa Tsöndrü Drakpa.

73 Tatsak Tsewang Gyal, *Dharma History*, 159–64.

74 In recent times Lama Shang's text was mostly known from the version included in Jamgön Kongtrul's *Treasury of Instructions*, which had numerous lines missing and two pages written out of order. Fortunately the version in his collected works is now readily available, and I am thankful to Dan Martin for supplying me a copy from his own collection when this translation was made. Only later did I learn that Dan's own translation of this text was published as "A Twelfth-Century Classic of Mahāmudrā: The Path of Ultimate Profundity: The Great Seal Instructions of Zhang" in *The Journal of the International Association of Buddhist Studies* 15.2 (1992): 243–319.

75 In praises, the lasso is a common metaphor for the power of the buddhas' blessing and compassion, with which the buddhas can lasso beings and so rescue them from suffering.

76 This refers to elaborate rituals where various images are made, though most commonly these are made from dough. Particular wooden blocks with a series of molds upon them are used to make a wide variety of representations for ritual use.

77 This does not mean heat literally, and it is not a reference to *caṇḍālī* practice, which has heat as a sign of its success, but is an expression for signs that one is progressing on the spiritual path toward enlightenment. It specifically refers to signs of being on the first stage of the path of engagement, the second of the five paths. The

analogy is of heat that comes from rubbing sticks together, indicating that one is on the way to creating fire.

78 Aconite is a deadly poison, but it was believed that peacocks were not only immune to poison, it is what produced the iridescent colors of their feathers.

79 The kāya of seven aspects is described by Dakpo Tashi Namgyal, quoting Vāgiśvarakīrti, in Roberts, *Mahāmudrā and Related Instructions*, 609–10. See there for more detail. Briefly, the aspects are saṃbhogakāya, union, great bliss, naturelessness, compassion, continuousness, ceaselessness.

80 *Sākarajñānavāda* in Sanskrit, this is a subschool of the Mind Only (Cittamātra) school. Its name derives from the assertion that the "aspects" (ākara, or *rnam pa* in Tibetan) of consciousness are real in that they are an integral part of the perceiving subject.

81 *Nirākārajñānavāda* in Sanskrit, this is another subschool of the Mind Only school. For Non-Aspectarians, the "aspects" of consciousness are unreal; they are mere concepts constructed by the mind and not an integral part of the perceiving subject.

82 The Māyāvāda school (*sgyu ma smra ba*). The division of the classical Indian Middle Way, or Madhyamaka, school into the Proponents of Illusion and the Utterly Nonabiding appears to have been quite common before Candrakīrti's writings came to dominate the Tibetan tradition around the late twelfth and early thirteenth centuries. Subsequently, the division of Madhyamaka into Svātrantika and Prāsaṅgika became the norm.

83 Apratiṣṭha (*rab tu mi gnas*).

84 The seven branches of practice are prostrating, offering, confessing, rejoicing, requesting to turn the wheel of Dharma, requesting not to go to nirvana, and dedicating.

85 Tib. *tshogs kyi 'khor lo*. "Circular gathering" is the original meaning, and in India a gaṇacakra feast was held in charnel grounds, with the consumption of the five meats and five nectars. In Tibet, general food and drink are blessed, and the participants, visualized as deities, consume them.

86 Tib. *byin bsregs*. The fire offering was a central feature in the traditions based on the Vedas and Brahmanas and had no place in

early Buddhism. Well-known pracitioners of homa threw away their implements in a gesture of renunciation on becoming disciples of the Buddha. However in the tantra, the offering to Agni, the deity of fire, is a prelude to offering to the *yidam* deities, and different shapes of hearth, offerings, color of costumes, and so on will bring the accomplishment that is either peaceful, increasing, controlling, or wrathful.

87 From the Sanskrit *sāccha*, miniature clay molds of stupas, deities, and the like. The Tibetan spelling and pronunciation varies between *satsa* and *tsatsa*.

88 *Bdud rtsi*, *amṛta*; the Vajrayāna inner offerings: human feces, urine, menstrual blood, flesh, and semen. The text here has an even more oblique synonym that reads literally as: "the half of ten deathless," as the Sanskrit *amṛta* means "without death."

89 Faith, diligence, mindfulness, samādhi, and wisdom.

90 Literally, don't [completely] cover your own head.

91 Milarepa's pupil Rechungpa (1084–1161). After leaving Milarepa he was principally based in the region of Loro, near the present-day border with Arunachal Pradesh, and therefore became known as Loro.

92 See Roberts, *Mahāmudrā and Related Instructions*, 590–93.

93 Tib. *Dkar po chig thub*, literally "white single powerful": a remedy—in this case the mahāmudrā realization of the nature of reality—that is sufficient in itself for the attainment of enlightenment.

94 *Bar do, anantarabhava*. An intermediate state of being that primarily refers to the period between death and rebirth but can also in certain specific contexts be applied more widely.

95 An alternate name for the Sūtrayāna or Perfection Vehicle (Parāmitāyāna).

96 Skt. *panasa*; the jackfruit can be eaten when it is unripe.

97 *Shes rab ye shes, prajñā-jñāna*. In the third empowerment, one gains wisdom (*jñāna*) through union with the consort (*prajñā*).

98 A corruption of the Sanskrit *iti*; can be loosely translated as "thus." It normally follows the conclusion of a title, quotation, and the like.

99 Tatsak Tsewang Gyal, *Dharma History*, 645–63; Gö Lotsāwa, *Blue Annals*, 664–70.

100 For further information see Michael Aris, *Bhutan: The Early History of a Himalayan Kingdom* (Warminster, England: Aris and Phillips, 1979).

101 *Dkar brgyud,* "white lineage," a reference to the white cotton robes worn by repas. A phonological development from the more common and original Kagyü (*bka' brgyud*), "instruction lineage."

102 *Enlightenment of Vairocana* (*Mahāvairocanābhisambodhi*). Though the passage describing the posture is on 195b, these lines do not appear in the text.

103 Saraha, *Treasury of Dohas* (*Dohakoṣagīti*), 74a3.

104 These noncanonical but well-known lines may have their first appearance in Gampopa, *Ornament of Precious Liberation*, 187a1. However, that early version is "Do not contemplate, do not think, do not know, / do not meditate, do not analyze, but rest naturally."

105 One of the names used for Gampopa, referring to his previous life as the principal interlocutor in the *King of Samādhis Sutra*.

106 The source of the quotation has not been identified. However, a fuller form of the quotation is given by the 68th Je Khenpo, Tenzin Dönkun Drupai Dé in *The Excellent Path*, 10b5 (611a): "Nondistraction is the path of all the buddhas. Nondistraction is the spiritual friend. Nondistraction is the chief of all instructions."

107 *Letter to a Friend* (*Suhṛllekha*), 43a5.

108 Vasubandhu, *Treatise on the Five Aggregates* (*Pañcaskandhaprakaraṇa*), 12b7. The original text begins with *dran pa gang zhe na*: "What is mindfulness?"

109 A four-line prayer that all beings attain to the state of the guru in his aspects as the buddha, the dharmakāya, the sambhogakāya, and the nirmāṇakāya.

110 *Treasury of the Ultimate*, 12b5.

111 The epithet "lord of yoga" or "lord of yogins," though often used as a reference to Milarepa, is in the Drukpa Kagyü context, as here, an epithet fot Lingrepa. See also note 122.

112 *Collected Works of Lingchen Repa Pema Dorjé*, vol. 1, 20a6.

113 *Treasury of Dohas* (*Dohakoṣagīti*), 23a5.

114 The hide of the elephant is too thick for thorns to have any effect.

115 Maitreyanātha, *Mahāyanasūtrālaṃkāra*, 15:15, 19a7.

116 Source unidentified. The only well-known master named *Rgyal ba'i dbang po* is Jinendrabuddhi, the teacher of Dignaga. However, this verse does not appear in his works, nor does it seem likely to be authored by him. As an epithet, this is most likely to refer to the Second Drukchen, Kunga Paljor.

117 *Entering the Conduct of a Bodhisattva* (*Bodhicaryāvatāra*), 5:41, 11b6.

118 *Kāśyapa Chapter* (*Kāśyapaparivartasūtra*), 133b1. The Kangyur version ends: "...and burns up the discriminating thoughts."

119 *Treasury of Dohas* (*Dohakoṣagīti*), 73b5.

120 Ibid., 71b3.

121 Ibid., 72a3.

122 The epithet "lord of yoga" here refers to Lingrepa. Lingrepa is named as the source of this quotation in other Drukpa Kagyu texts, with the additional initial line "In the nature of the mind that is without basis or root." Also Pema Karpo used this epithet above (see note 111) in attributing a different quotation to Lingrepa.

123 *Treasury of Dohas* (*Dohakoṣagīti*), 72a2. Though this quote may, like the preceding one, appear to also be attributed to "the lord of yoga," it is from Saraha.

124 Ibid., 71b2.

125 Ibid., 74b7. "The Lord" refers to the Buddha.

126 The variant Tillipa is used here, and Tailo is used in the version on page 106 (see above in same text).

127 This noncanonical song appears in Wangchuk Gyaltsen's *Great Bliss of Stainless Teachings*, vol. 1, 58a1.

128 Pema Karpo already quoted these lines above. See note 104.

129 Specifically, attachment to the experiences of clarity, bliss, and no thought.

130 The royal capital of Zangskar, a Tibetan region in Kashmir, was at the town of Padum.

131 *Mkhar chu byang chub kyi snying po*. Kharchu at Lhodrak. The retreat place of Padmasambhava's mind, within a day's walk from Marpa's residence in Lhodrak.

132 Gö Lotsāwa, *Blue Annals*, 476.

133 A history of the Karmapas is found in Thinley, *History of the Sixteen Karmapas.*

134 His name is spelled Telopa throughout this text, the most common Tibetan spelling of his name.

135 Maitreyanātha, *Mahāyānasūtrālaṃkāra*, 14:13, 18a4.

136 *Hevajratantra*, book 2, 2:51, 16a4.

137 Maitreyanātha, *Madhyāntavibhāga*, 1a4. Objectlessness, literally "nonperception" (*mi dmigs pa, dmigs pa med pa*; *anupalabdhi* or *anupalambha*), is also translated as "nonreferentiality." It is in effect a synonym for emptiness.

138 Tailikapāda (Tilopa), *Mahāmudrā Instructions (Mahāmudropadeśa)*, 243b3.

139 *Treasury of Dohas (Dohakoṣagīti)*, 72b7.

140 *Eight-Thousand-Verse Perfection of Wisdom Sutra (Aṣṭasāhasrikāprajñāpāramitā)*, chap. 8, 111a2.

141 Text unidentified.

142 Wangchuk Gyaltsen, *Great Bliss of Stainless Teachings: A Biography of Nāropa*, 58a1.

143 Rangjung Dorjé in his *Treatise Differentiating Consciousnesses and Wisdom* (p. 270) ascribes the view of "fate" (*phywa*) to Bön, atoms to the Vaibhāṣika view, unperceivable externals to the Sautrāntika view, and the puruṣa (literally "individual") to the view of the non-Buddhist Sāṃkhya.

144 Saraha, *Treasury of Dohas (Dohakoṣagīti)*, 75b2.

145 Ibid., 72a5. The second line does not appear in the Tengyur version.

146 Nāropa, *Dṛṣṭisaṃkṣipta*, 244b3. No author is named in any edition of the canon. The translator is Marpa Chökyi Lodrö, Nāropa's pupil, but it is also grouped among nine Tilopa texts. However, later on in this work, Rangjung Dorjé attributes this text to Nāropa.

147 Śāntideva, *Entering the Conduct of a Bodhisattva (Bodhicaryāvatāra)*, 8:4, 23b2.

148 The ten signs of luminosity are smoke, mirage, clouds, fireflies, sun, moon, shining jewels, eclipse, stars, and light rays.

149 The two experiences of clarity are the clarity of the five senses and the clarity of the mind, as described above.

150 The "immediate condition" (*de ma thag pa'i rkyen, anantara-pratyaya*), as found in Asaṅga's *Compendium of the Abhidharma* (*Abhidharmasamuccaya*), was applied by Rangjung Dorjé, particularly in his text *Distinguishing between Wisdoms and Consciousnesses* as "the immediate mentation" (*de ma thag pa'i yid*), a subdivision of the seventh consciousness, the "afflicted-mentation consciousness" (*nyon yid rnam shes, kliṣṭamanasvijñāna*).

151 While good and bad karma bring happiness and suffering in the desire realm, the act of meditation can have the karmic result of rebirth in the form and formless realms.

152 The third of the five paths of accumulation, engagement, seeing, meditation, and no-more training. The path of seeing is the threshold to becoming an ārya being and, in the Mahayana, to embarking on the ten bodhisattva levels.

153 These four meditation states are also the four dhyāna levels of the formless realm.

154 *Satkāyadṛṣṭi* ("the view of the existent body"), the view that the five aggregates are a self. This was freely translated into Tibetan as *'jig tshogs lta ba*, which in English would be "the view of the perishable aggregate or transitory collection."

155 Unidentified. Elsewhere the second is called *Four Connections of View and Meditation*.

156 *Mahāmudrā Instructions* (*Mahāmudropadeśa*), 243b5.

157 *Summary of the View* (*Dṛṣṭisaṃkṣipta*), 245b1.

158 Source unidentified.

159 *Summary of the View* (*Dṛṣṭisaṃkṣipta*), 245b1. It immediately follows and contrasts with the previously quoted verse from this text.

160 These five kinds of adverse factors are unidentified.

161 Gampopa. The text is unidentified.

162 Dechen Teng, Rangjung Dorjé's retreat center above Tsurphu Monastery.

163 Situ Tenpai Nyinjé, "Oral Transmission of the Supreme Siddhas," in Roberts, *Mahāmudrā and Related Instructions*, 175–288. Also,

Sherab Dorje, *The Eighth Situpa on the Third Karmapa's Maha-mudra Prayer* (Ithaca, NY: Snow Lion, 2004).

164 An earlier translation of this text was published as *The Lamp of Mahamudra* (Boston: Shambhala, 1989).

165 *Guhyagarbhatantra*, chap. 5, 115a5.

166 *Treasury of Dohas (Dohakoṣagīti)*, 72b5.

167 The Cittamātra or Yogācāra school taught three natures: *imagi-nary (kun tu btags pa, parikalpita)*, which is an object of cognition that is purely conceptual; *dependent (gzhan dbang, paratantra)*, the nonconceptual cognition of dependently arisen phenomena; and *absolute (yongs su grub pa, pariniṣpanna)*, the direct percep-tion of the nature of the mind. The *absolute* is taught to have two aspects: changeless and irreversible. See Jamgön Kongtrul Lodrö Thayé, *The Treasury of Knowledge, book 6, part 3: Frameworks of Buddhist Philosophy* (Ithaca, NY: Snow Lion, 2007), 175–94. Also, Dan Lusthaus, *Buddhist Phenomenology: A Philosophical Investigation of Yogācāra* (London: Routledge Curzon, 2002), and Fernando Tola and Carmen Dragonetti, *Being as Conscious-ness: Yogācāra Philosophy of Buddhism* (Delhi: Motilal Banarsi-dass, 2006).

168 Gyalwa Yangönpa, *The Great Tantra that Teaches Unimpeded Dzogchen*, 15a3.

169 This is in reference to the Yogācāra's doctrine of three natures. See note 167 above.

170 This is simply the lack of attachment one has to something that one dislikes.

171 *Hevajratantra*, book 2, 4:70, 22b3.

172 Maitreyanātha, *Mahāyānottaranatraśāstra*, 1:51, 57a2.

173 *Praise to the Dharmadhātu (Dharmadhātustava)*, v. 37, 65a3.

174 Sudhana studied under a succession of many teachers, culminat-ing in Maitreya, in the *Gaṇḍhavyūha Sutra*, which is the final section of the *Avataṃsaka Sutra*. The story of Sadāprarudita's hardships and dedication in search of the teachings is given in chapter 30 of the *Eight-Thousand-Verse Perfection of Wisdom Sutra (Aṣṭasāhasrikāprajñāpāramitā)*.

175 Dampa Sangye, *The Essence of a Precious Portion of the Tantras,*

6b3. The text had erroneously cited a similarly named Nyingma tantra.

176 Saraha, *Dohakoṣagīti*, 71b2.

177 Source unidentified.

178 Lorepa Darma Wangchuk (1187–1250) was the founder of the lower, or eastern, Drukpa tradition. The source of the quotation has not been identified.

179 Source unidentified.

180 Source unidentified.

181 Source unidentified.

182 *Daśacakrakṣitigarbhasūtra*. This quotation has not been found in this sutra, though a similar passage commences on folio 191b1.

183 This quotation has not been found in either the Pacification or Cakrasaṃvara tantras of that name. Also, no reference to them have been located in the works of Gampopa. The four verses here draw a direct parallel between the four yogas of mahāmudrā and the four stages of the path of engagement, the second of the five paths.

184 *Gnad kyi zin tig.* The text has not been identified.

185 The source of the quotation has not been identified. It is not among any of Niguma's known works or biographies.

186 *Samādhirājasūtra*, 100b6.

187 *Avataṃsakasūtra,* vol. *kha,* 186a5. This level is the first of the ten bodhisattva levels. These are the "five fears of the bodhisattva on the paths of accumulation and engagement."

188 The perfection of wisdom sutras.

189 The third level is missing from the available editions of the *Bright Torch*.

190 The three powers of the body (*lus kyi rtsal gsum*) are said to be the ability to press down flesh with a finger, to swim across a great river, and to have powerful lightness, like a bird. There are also three powers of the speech and the mind.

191 A very common phrase, but this text inexplicably has the nonsensical opposite: "liberated in one through knowing all."

192 The three kinds of emanations are (1) those that are emanated—without being born—in order to accomplish a certain deed at

a certain time and place, (2) those that are born like ordinary humans, and (3) the supreme emanation, which is a buddha.

193 The Tibetan text has the explanatory annotations of "ordinary beings" for thickly obscured, "yogins" for partially obscured, and "buddhas" for unobscured.

194 The Tibetan text has explanatory additions, which appear rather forced: "The worldly is the wrong path, the tīrthika is the mistaken path, the śrāvaka and pratyekabuddha are the erroneous path, and the lower tantras the bondage."

195 *Udumbara.* The fig tree never has flowers. It has also in Tibet been taken to refer to a mythical flower that only blossoms when a cakravartin or Buddha is born.

196 Explanatory additions to the Tibetan edition specify that the first line describes the view, the second line describe the meditation, the third line describes the conduct, and the fourth line describes the result.

197 Literally, one that has had warmth and grease removed. A more common but slightly different metaphor involving intractable leather is that of used butter bags, as butter can no longer soften it, exemplifying a mind that has become impervious to the Dharma through unskillful overexposure to it.

198 The anonymous Tibetan annotations state that the first line describes those who are incapable of meditation, the second line describes those who do not believe in meditation, and the third line describes those who do not understand the essential point of meditation.

199 "Descending to the water goddess" means setting over the sea, and the vermilion clouds are the red clouds of sunset.

200 No information is currently available about Mengom Tsultrim Sangpo. Tselé Natsok Rangdröl also wrote an eleven-folio work entitled *Answers to Mengom's Questions* (*Sman sgom gyi dris lan gnyis chos zung 'jug gi ngo sprod zhal gdams*) in which he is referred to as "the supreme vidyādhara of Mengom" (1b1) and as "Tsultrim Rinchen, the great meditator of Men" (*sman sgom chen tshul khrims rin chen*) (11b4).

201 That is, *Instructions for the Mahāmudrā Innate Union*, the text by Rangjung Dorjé earlier in this volume.

202 *Yi ge bzhi pa.* A teaching on: (1) understanding the basis of the *mind*, (2) methods for following the path of *meditation*, (3) cutting through errors in the *view*, (4) transforming [everything] into the path through *conduct*.

203 Tilopa, *Mahāmudrā Instructions* (*Mahāmudropadeśa*). A song by Tilopa to Nāropa delivered on the banks of the Ganges and therefore popularly known as the "Ganges Mahāmudrā."

204 Kamalaśīla, *Letterless Mahāmudrā* (*Mahāmudrātattvānākṣaropadeśa*).

205 Direct introduction to the nature of the mind through symbols.

206 Introduced into Tibet by Vajrapāṇi (b. 1017), who was a pupil of Maitripa.

207 These teachings are said to be based on the *Cakrasaṃvara Tantra of the Inconceivable Secret* (*Cakrasaṃvaraguhyācintyatantra*).

208 Mahāmudrā through the fourth, or word, empowerment.

209 The fivefold mahāmudrā tradition of the Drigung Kagyü, the five aspects being: (1) bodhicitta, (2) deity meditation, (3) guru devotion, (4) the nonconceptual view, and (5) dedication. The fourth is itself also called *mahāmudrā*, but all five are taught to be aspects of mahāmudrā.

210 *Wish-Fulfilling Jewel of Mind Instructions* (*Sems khrid yid bzhin nor bu*), which were received by Tilopa from ḍākinīs.

211 *Gnad gyi gzer drug.* A teaching given by Tilopa: "Do not contemplate, do not think, do not know, / do not meditate, do not analyze, but rest naturally." See note 104.

212 *Vast Expanse Free from Extremes* is from Sangyé Lingpa's *Unity of the Gurus' Realization*. *Sun's Essence* is from Ratna Lingpa. The *Single Knowing* is the instruction on the all-inclusive knowledge. *Dispelling the Darkness of Ignorance* is the practice of luminosity in the daytime and in sleep. *Seeing the Naked Intrinsic Nature* is from Ngari Tertön Garwang Dorjé.

213 A.k.a. Götsangpa Natsok Rangdröl. Here he distinguishes himself from Götsangpa Gönpo Dorjé, the well-known Drukpa Kagyü master. Götsang means "vulture nest." Both Tselé Natsok

Rangdröl and Gönpo Dorjé gained their epithets through dwelling at identically named caves, the former in Palri and the latter in Latö. The early sixteenth-century Götsang Repa, also known as Natsok Rangdröl, has sometimes been confused with both of these Götsangpas.

Glossary

.

Abhidharma (*mngon pa'i chos*). This set of teachings attempts to give an analytic overview of the foundation and worldview of Buddhism. It is primarily concerned with the constituents of mental activity and their relationship to the process of attaining enlightenment, but it also includes descriptions of cosmology and the constituents of the external world. In Tibet, the texts of Vasubandhu and Asaṅga form the basis for the study of Abhidharma.

ācārya (*slob dpon*). This is a traditional Indian title denoting a person of superior knowledge, spiritual training, or position.

accumulation of merit and wisdom. *See* two accumulations.

aggregates (*phung po, skandha*). The five psychophysical constituents of an individual: form, sensations, identifications, mental actions, and consciousnesses.

Akaniṣṭha (*'og min*). Literally, "highest." This is the highest paradise in the form realm and thus the highest physical residence in samsara. It became further elevated in the yoga tantras as the abode of Vairocana and the source of the yoga tantras. In the highest yoga tantras it is the abode of the ultimate Buddha Vajradhara and is entirely outside samsara.

ālaya (*kun gzhi*) and **ālaya consciousness** (*kun gzhi rnam shes, ālayavijñāna*). Literally *ālaya* means a dwelling or abode, as in Himālaya, the "abode of snows." It is translated into Tibetan as *kun gzhi*, which means "basis of everything." However, it primarily relates to the separate mind or continuum of an individual and not a shared universal foundation. The concept existed in early Buddhism as an explanation of why an individual does not cease to exist when consciousness stops and was termed *bhavaṅga* in the Theravāda tradition. The *ālaya* later became an explanation, particularly in the Cittamātra tradition, for where karmic seeds are stored and was considered the source of an individual's mentally produced experiences. It is usually synonymous with the *ālaya consciousness*, which is the neutral basis for samsara and which ceases upon liberation.

ārya (*'phags pa*). "Noble one." This term is applied to those who have reached the path of seeing on whichever vehicle they follow. In terms of the Mahayana path it is synonymous with bodhisattvas.

asuras (*lha ma yin*). Demigods jealous of the status of the devas. In Tibet asuras are of little cultural importance, only appearing in the classification of the six classes of beings. When the classes of beings are enumerated as five, they are omitted.

Avalokiteśvara (*spyan ras gzigs*). The bodhisattva of compassion.

Avīci (*mnar med*). The worst and physically lowest of the hells, where beings remain longer and suffer greater than any other hell.

āyatana (*skye mched*). The Tibetan literally means "arise and increase," while the Sanskrit means "base" or "source." The term is used variously but most commonly for the six organs of perception—which includes the mental faculty—and their perceived objects. It may also refer to the various states of perception in the formless realms.

Bhagavān (*bcom ldan 'das*). An epithet for the Buddha.

bindu (*thig le*). Generally *bindu* means a spot or a drop. As a quintessence, it is a distillation of the essential essence or character of something. In the context of tantric physiognomy, it refers to subtle physical essences traveling within the channels or to grosser secretions.

bodhicitta (*byang chub sems*). Most commonly, in a Mahayana context, this refers to the intention to become enlightened so that one may free all beings from samsara, an intention that can be either merely aspirational or actively engaged. This *relative bodhicitta* is sometimes contrasted with *ultimate bodhicitta*, the mind of a buddha, which is free of all misconceptions. Within the higher tantras *bodhicitta* can also be a euphemism for semen.

bodhisattva (*byang chub sems dpa'*). The term can technically be applied to anyone who has taken the bodhisattva vow to attain buddhahood in order to benefit beings, but it usually refers to the deity-like beings who have reached the bodhisattva levels (*bhūmi*).

cakravartin (*'khor los sgyur ba'i rgyal po*). An exalted sovereign with universal dominion. The name means "roller of a wheel." In the earliest sutras, cakravartins were mythical kings. On becoming king, they set a magical wheel rolling and wherever it went became their lands; for some it would roll throughout the world.

Cārvāka (*rgyang 'phen pa*). A school of thought whose members denied that a god or karma created the world or that there is a life after death.

central channel (*dbu ma*, *avadhūtī*). The main passageway for the winds within the body's subtle physiology, which is manipulated in tantric practice. It runs parallel to the spine.

channel (*rtsa*, *nāḍī*). This generally refers to the network of subtle channels, analogous to the nervous system, through which flow the winds that are mentally manipulated as part of tantric practice.

Cittamātra (*sems tsam*). This school—also known as Yogācāra—propounded the view that all phenomena are merely manifestations of the mind, which alone is ultimately real. The school grew out of the teachings of Asaṅga and Vasubandhu in the fourth century and is one of two main philosophical traditions of Mahayana Buddhism alongside the Madhyamaka.

conqueror (*rgyal ba, jina*). The most common term used to refer to the buddhas in Tibetan. Capitalized, it refers to the Buddha. Its etymology refers to being victorious over one's own ignorance and defects.

ḍākinī (*mkha' 'gro ma*). As with the ḍākas, earlier Indian and Buddhist literature represent ḍākinīs as malevolent devourers of humans. This aspect still survives as the class of ḍākinīs known as *flesh eaters*. In the antinomian higher tantras, these creatures became guardians of secret teachings. *Wisdom ḍākinīs* (*jñānaḍākinī*) are those who have attained buddhahood and manifest in the form of a ḍākinī in order to benefit beings. Similarly women who are enlightened, especially if they are not ordained, are known as ḍākinīs, including the mothers and consorts of lamas.

degenerate age (*snyigs ma'i dus*). The era during which five degeneracies (*snyigs ma, kaṣāya*) occur: lifespan, beings, afflictions, views, and the era.

dependent origination (*rten cing 'brel 'byung, pratītyasamutpāda*). The teaching that nothing exists independently. It is often systematized in a teaching on twelve interdependent links, whereby all of samsara comes about in dependence on the first link, ignorance.

devas (*lha*). A general term for any god or deity, but it is particularly associated with the gods in Indian mythology who possessed the *amrita*, or nectar of immortality, that the asuras kept trying to steal, without success. By extension it refers to any being who has been reborn in a samsaric paradise.

Dharma (*chos*). In Buddhist texts, this most often refers to the teachings of the Buddha, which are exalted for their power to liberate from suffering. In Sanskrit this is the general term for "truth" or "religion," but it has many meanings. Frequently, it refers simply to an existent or an object of the mind.

Dharma wheel (*chos kyi 'khor lo, dharmacakra*). This metaphor from the early sutras comes from comparing the Buddha to a cakravartin king. Buddha is said to have turned his wheel of Dharma instead of secular power. In the Mahayana, there are said to be three "turnings" of the wheel of Dharma corresponding to three levels of teachings in the scriptures. The first is the general teachings shared with the śrāvakas and pratyekabuddhas. The second, exemplified by the Perfection of Wisdom sutras, presents the explanation of emptiness. And the third expounds buddha nature. *See also* cakravartin.

dharmadhātu (*chos kyi dbyings*). This term can mean the entire expanse of phenomena but also the "essential element" of phenomena, which is emptiness, or an indivisible union of emptiness and fundamental clarity.

dharmakāya (*chos sku*). The "truth body" of a buddha, in contradistinction to a buddha's corporeal form body (*rūpakāya*). *Dharmakāya* originally referred to the teachings themselves, which remained as the Buddha's presence or body even after his form body was gone. As the term evolved, it came to be a synonym for ultimate reality, or emptiness, and the realization of these in the mind of a buddha.

dhyāna (*bsam gtan*). Synonymous with *samādhi* and *śamatha*, it means "placed" and "fixed" and is etymologically a form of the *dhi* in *samādhi*. The closest translation would be "concentration," for it means the mind fixed upon a point without deviation, but in a less technical context could simply be called meditation.

drop (*thig le*). *See* bindu.

eight worldly concerns (*'jig rten chos brgyad*). Concern with various kinds of pleasure and displeasure, specifically gain and loss, pleasure and pain, praise and blame, fame and obscurity.

elaboration (*spros pa, prapañca*). The tendency of thoughts to multiply in discursive wandering. The Sanskrit word can mean expansion, diffusion, or diversification, and also covers prolixity, creation, and deceit. "Conceptual" is sometimes added to the English to better communicate the meaning.

embellishment (*sgro btags*). Reified concepts, which conceive something to be other than what it is, such as the assumption of permanence.

emptiness (*stong pa nyid, śūnyatā*). This concept developed in Mahayana Buddhism to denote the absence of any real nature to phenomena; it is the central philosophical tenet of the Madhyamaka presentation of reality.

five kinds of visions (*spyan lnga, pañcacakṣus*). These are ordinary vision, divine vision, wisdom vision, Dharma vision, and buddha vision.

form realm (*gzugs khams, rūpadhātu*). A set of seventeen paradises into which beings are born through the power of meditation.

formless realm (*gzugs med khams, arūpadhātu*). A set of four existences that are states of meditation that a being who dies in one of those four states is born into.

freedoms and wealths (*dal 'byor*). This refers to the "precious human existence," which is free from eight states that prevent being able to practice the Dharma: being born in hell, as a preta, as an animal, as a long-living deva, in a time when a Buddha has not come, as a "savage" (i.e., in a land without the Dharma), having wrong views, and having impaired faculties. The wealths are five derived from oneself: being human, in a land with the Dharma, having all one's faculties, not having done the worst karmic deeds, and having faith. The second five are from others: a Buddha has come, he has taught, the teachings remain, the teachings have followers, and there is a teacher that guides us.

garuda (*khyung, garuḍa*). Mythical supreme bird; the enemy of serpents, with a divine semihuman form.

gongpo (*'gong po*). A class of demons who can influence people into doing wrong or becoming obsessed with wealth, power, and so on.

highest yoga tantra (*bla na med pa'i rgyud, anuttarayogatantra*). One of the terms used for such tantras as Guhyasamāja and Cakrasaṃvara as they began to become prevalent from the eighth century onward.

innate union (*lhan cig skye sbyor, sahajayoga*). Sometimes rendered as "coemergent" or "connate" union, *innate union* means to become united with the natural state that is innate in the mind, or connate with everything that arises within it.

kāya (*sku*). A "body" of a buddha that manifests his or her enlightened qualities. Earlier Buddhist texts speak only of two kāyas, a form body (*rūpakāya*) and a formless *dharmakāya*, or "truth body." Later, the form body was divided into two to produce the well-known classification of the three kāyas of a buddha: saṃbhogakāya, nirmāṇakāya, and dharmakāya. One also finds additional divisions to produce lists of four or five kāyas.

knowing (*rig pa, vidyā*). *Vidyā* is the general name for knowledge, as in branches of knowledge and the mind's cognition in general, but gains deeper meaning by context, especially the nonconceptual knowing nature of the mind.

level (*sa, bhūmi*). Most often, the graduated levels of enlightenment that a bodhisattva passes through to attain buddhahood. Frequently enumerated as ten, they can also be expanded to include the level of buddhahood and two lower levels that correspond to the paths of accumulation and engagement, making thirteen in all.

lifetime vows (*gtan khrims*). This can refer to either the lay or monastic vows. When they are specified as five in number, they are the lay vows (*dge bsnyen, upāsaka*): (1) not to kill, (2) not to steal, (3) not to lie, (4) either celibacy or not to have sexual misconduct, and (5) not to take intoxicants.

luminosity (*'od gsal, prabhāsvara*). The Tibetan means "clear light," whereas the Sanskrit may more correctly be translated as "brightness." Luminosity is too soft a word, but it has gained common usage to describe this vivid aspect of the nature of the mind in contradistinction to its emptiness.

Madhyamaka (*dbu ma*). "Middle Way." The philosophical tradition descending from Nāgārjuna, which propounds a middle way between the extremes of existence and nonexistence. All schools of Tibetan Buddhism follow this tradition, though they differ on the exact interpretation of the Madhyamaka view.

mandala (*dkyil 'khor, maṇḍala*). This may refer to any circle or circular arrangement, but in Buddhism it most frequently refers to an arrangement of deities, with a central deity in the center and including the palace they are situated within. To "offer a mandala" is to ritually make an offering of the entire universe with visualizations and prayers enumerating its contents.

Mantrayāna (*gsang sngags theg pa*). The "way of mantra"; a synonym for tantra, the esoteric vehicle of Mahayana Buddhism.

māra (*bdud*). The Sanskrit literally means "death." In the early sutras Māra is a deity that continually tries to stop the Buddha's enlightenment and the spread of his teachings. Māras more generally are personifications of one's obstacles to enlightenment.

meditation and post-meditation (*mnyam bzhags* and *rjes thob, samāhita* and *pṛṣṭhalabdha*). *Samāhita* is actually the past participle of the verb *samādha* from which comes the noun *samādhi* and is likewise a general name for a state of meditation. *Pṛṣṭhalabdha* or *rjes thob* is literally "post-accomplishment" but rendered here as *post-meditation*.

The "accomplishment" refers to the accomplishment of meditation and so refers to the period when, having obtained those qualities, they are put to use in daily life by teaching and benefiting beings. In Tibet, the word was also interpreted to mean the accomplishment of realization while not in a meditation session.

Mind Only. *See* Cittamātra.

nāga (*klu*). Literally "cobra." These serpents are considered to have a divine form and to live in an underground or underwater world.

nirmāṇakāya (*sprul pa'i sku*). One of the two form bodies (*rūpakāya*) of a buddha. The "emanation body" is the form of a buddha that appears in this world, perceivable by other beings, in contradistinction to the *saṃbhogakāya*, which can only be seen by enlightened beings. The idea of nirmāṇakāya was also extended to emanations that are not obviously a buddha: seemingly ordinary beings, animals, and even matter, such as bridges, boats, food, or whatever would assist beings. The Tibetan translation *tulku* has also become institutionalized to mean anyone who is recognized as the rebirth of a lama.

nirvana (*mya ngan las 'das pa, nirvāṇa*). Nirvana comes from the term "to blow out," as in extinguishing a candle, and therefore means "extinguishment" or even "extinction" in the sense of ending the succession of lifetimes and their cause. The Tibetan interpretative translation means "transcending misery."

obscuration. *See* two obscurations.

one-day vows (*bsnyen gnas, upavāsa*). Intended for lay people, these vows are taken for twenty-four hours. They are (1) not to kill, (2) not to steal, (3) not to lie, (4) not to have sexual activity, (5) not to take intoxicants, (6) not to eat after noon, (7) not to sit on a high seat, and (8) not to dance or wear adronments and perfumes.

paṇḍita. A title given to an individual recognized for his or her learning. It has entered the English language as pundit.

Perfection Vehicle (*phar phyin theg pa, pāramitāyāna*). "The yāna of the [six] perfections" is an alternative name for the Mahayana's sutra tradition.

perfections (*pāramitā, pha rol tu phyin pa*). *See* six perfections.

pratyekabuddha (*rang rgyal*). Often paired with *śrāvakas* ("disciples") as one of two Lesser Vehicle paths, these individuals attained buddhahood without recourse to a teacher.

preta (*yi dwags*). One of the six classes of existence, these beings suffer from relentless hunger and thirst.

primary and secondary signs. These are the signs, or marks, of a great being. There are thirty-two primary and eighty secondary features. The Buddha is said to have had all these features.

propensity (*bag chags, vāsana*). The Sanskrit term is derived from a scent or smell left behind and therefore has the meaning of a trace or impression. The Tibetan has an emphasis on habitual action, or even the apparently instinctive, such as the first actions of a newborn animal. It can also have the meaning of a seed, a latent tendency to act in a certain way, or even, in the Mind Only school, that which causes one's apparently external experiences, as these are said to arise entirely from one's own mind.

quintessence. *See* bindu.

Śākyamuni (*shā kya thub pa*). The Buddha, the "sage of the Śākya clan."

samādhi (*ting nge 'dzin*). This could literally be translated as "concentration," meaning when the mind is completely focused. It therefore refers to a state of meditation free from distraction. *See also* dhyāna.

Sarma (*gsar ma*). Literally "new," this contrasts with the "old" or Nyingma (*rnying ma*) tradition. The Sarma traditions are based on teachings that were brought to Tibet from the eleventh century onward, beginning with the translations of Lotsāwa Rinchen Sangpo.

Sautrantika (*mdo sde pa*). The "followers of the sutras," an Indian Buddhist tradition that rejected the canonical status of the Abhidharma. This tradition, like the Vaibhāṣikas, was within the Sarvastivāda school and continued developing through the first millennium.

self-knowing (*rang rig, svasaṃvedyā*). This can sometimes mean just one's own personal knowledge or perception. It is also particularly used, as in the Mind Only tradition, for consciousness perceiving itself.

six existences (*rigs drug*). The six types of existence in samsara are rebirth as a hell being, preta, animal, human, asura, or deva.

six perfections (*phar phyin drug, ṣaḍpāramitā*). The six central practices of a bodhisattva on the Mahayana path: the perfections of generosity, good conduct, patience, diligence, meditation, and wisdom.

śrāvaka (*nyan thos*). "Disciple." The Tibetan translation is "one who listens and hears." In early Buddhism the path of the śrāvaka was the direct path to liberation, while a bodhisattva, committed to becoming a buddha and not just free of samsara, had to accumulate merit for many eons. *See also* pratyekabuddha.

Śrāvaka Vehicle (*nyan thos theg pa, śrāvakayāna*). "The way of the disciples," a term that is often used as a synonym for the Lesser Vehicle in contrast with the Bodhisattva Vehicle of the Mahayana.

terma (*gter ma*). From the word for "treasure," *gter*, termas are discovered teachings, either practices concealed in the mind during a previous life or texts, artifacts, and substances discovered in physical form.

three realms (*khams gsum, traidhātu*). The desire realm, form realm, and formless realm. The desire realm includes all the six existences including some of the devas, such as those in the Tuṣita and Trāyastriṃśa paradises. The form-realm devas are more subtle in their forms and longer lived and find their highest abode in the paradise of Akaniṣṭha. Beings in the formless realm have no bodies and rest for thousands of eons in blissful samādhi.

tīrthikas (*mu stegs pa*). Tibetan uses this to refer to non-Buddhists, but those in the Indian tradition only.

torma (*gtor ma, bali*). *Torma* is Tibetan for a ritual offering cake usually made of barley flour and butter and often elaborately designed and subject to detailed explanations. The Indian precedent, the *bali*, was simply a baked circle of bread.

treatise (*bstan bcos, śāstra*). A general term for any work by a Buddhist author, in contrast to the sutras and tantras attributed to the Buddha himself.

triple aspects of conceptualization (*'khor gsum, trimaṇḍala*). The concepts of one who does an action, the action itself, and the object of the action.

two accumulations (*tshogs gnyis*). The dualistic accumulation of merit and the nondual "accumulation" of wisdom.

two obscurations (*sgrib gnyis, āvaraṇa*). The obscuration formed by the afflictions and the obscuration of knowledge. The latter is named according to what is obscured rather than by the cause of obscuration, the subtlest level of ignorance.

Vaibhāṣika (*bye brag tu smra ba*). Followers of a tradition based on a text commonly referred to as the *Vibhāsa*, which was a compilation of Abhidharma teachings.

vajra (*rdo rje*). The word *vajra* refers to the "thunderbolt," the indestructible and irresistible weapon that first appears in Indian literature in the hand of the Vedic deity Indra. In Tibetan Buddhism, *vajra* is most often used as a modifier to indicate something related to the tantric path, as it symbolizes the swiftness and power of that path and the indestructibility of the dharmakāya.

vajra body (*rdo rje'i sku, vajrakāya*). The physical body of a buddha.

Vajradhara (*rdo rje 'chang*). The saṃbhogakāya form in which the Buddha is said to have taught the tantras. In the Kagyü tradition he is also the personification of the dharmakāya, and the source from which the saṃbhogakāya deities manifest.

Vajrapāṇi (*phyag na rdo rje*). Vajrapāṇi is both a wrathful deity and a bodhisattva who represents enlightened power, not to be confused with the historical figure, born 1017, who is associated with the dissemination of mahāmudrā teachings in Tibet.

Vajrayāna (*rdo rje theg pa*). The "Vajra Vehicle" is the path of tantra, synonymous with the Mantrayāna.

vidyādhara (*rig 'dzin*). A class of superhuman beings with magical powers that, in its meaning of "knowledge holder," became in Tibetan an honorific address for a tantric master.

vidyāvrata (*rig pa brtul zhugs*). "Deliberate conduct of knowledge," a euphemism for openly maintaining a tantric lifestyle of wearing a tantric costume, having a consort, and so on.

wind (*rlung, vāyu*). The word *vāyu* can mean air or wind, or even the god of the air. In the context of the higher tantras it can simultaneously mean the external element of air, the breath, and the winds or energies that flow through the body that cause digestion, defecation, and so on. These grosser winds can be transformed into wisdom winds through completion-stage practices.

wisdom being (*ye shes sems dpa'*, *jñānasattva*). In deity meditation, the wisdom being is the actual deity itself, which is imagined to blend with the visualized deity in order to inspire the confidence that one actually is the deity.

yakṣa (*gnod sbyin*). Feminine: *yakṣī* or *yakṣiṇī*. A class of supernatural beings, often represented as the attendants of the god of wealth, but the term is also applied to spirits. Though generally portrayed as benevolent, the Tibetan translation means "harm giver," as they are also capable of causing harm.

yidam deity (*yi dam*). The Tibetan meaning is "commitment" but refers more accurately to the deity to which one has a commitment. The Sanskrit equivalent, *iṣṭadeva* or *iṣṭadevatā*, means "desired deity," emphasizing one's attraction to or choice of a deity.

yoga (*rnal 'byor*). Cognate with the English *yoke*, it has the meaning of "union." The Tibetan translated it as "united" (*'byor*) with the natural state (*rnal*). It is also translated as the active form *sbyor ba*, which conveys such meanings as "application," "practice," and "endeavor."

yoga tantras (*rnal 'byor rgyud*). This is the third of the four classes of tantras following the action (*kriyā*) and performance (*caryā*) tantras.

Yogācāra (*rnal sbyor spyod pa*). *See* Cittamātra.

yoginī (*rnal 'byor ma*). Though a term for a female practitioner, particularly a practitioner of the higher tantras, it is also designates the later highest tantras, which are said to emphasize wisdom over method.

Bibliography

Source Texts

In preparing these translations, reference was made to multiple editions of the individual texts, but the primary editions are those in the special anthology of key texts of the Kagyü school developed for *The Library of Tibetan Classics*:

> *Mnyam med bka'brgyud lugs kyi phyag rgya chen po dang 'brel ba'i chos skor* [*Mahāmudrā and Related Teachings of the Peerless Kagyü Tradition*]. Bod kyi gtsug lag gces btus series 5. New Delhi: Institute of Tibetan Classics, 2008. (ISBN 81-89165-05-4)

In that anthology, the present works appear as follows:

1. Zhang Brtson 'grus grags pa, *Phyag rgya chen po sgom ma mo chen po'i sngon 'gro dngos gzhi*, pp. 31–48.
2. Zhang Brtson 'grus grags pa, *Phyag rgya chen po lam zab mthar thug*, pp. 49–78.
3. 'Brug pa Padma dkar po, *Phyag chen gyu zin bris*, pp. 79–90.
4. Karma pa Rang byung rdo rje, *Phyag rgya chen po lhan cig skyes sbyor gyi khrid yid*, pp. 91–102.
5. Karma pa Rang byung rdo rje, *Nges don phyag rgya chen po'i smon lam*, pp. 103–6.
6. Rtse le Sna tshogs rang grol, *Phyag rgya chen po'i don yang dag pa rab tu gsal bar byed pa dri ma med pa'i sgron mo*, pp. 191–228.

Works Cited in the Texts

KANGYUR AND NYINGMA GYÜBUM
(CANONICAL SCRIPTURES)

Aphorisms. Udānavarga. Ched du brjod pa'i tshoms. Toh 326, mdo sde
  sa. 209b–253a7.

*Avataṃsaka Sutra. Avataṃsakasūtra. Sangs rgyas phal po che zhes bya ba
  shin tu rgyas pa chen po'i mdo.* Toh 44, phal chen *ka–a.*

Buddhakapāla Tantra. Sangs rgyas thod pa'i rgyud. Toh 424, rgyud *nga.*

*Cakrasaṃvara Tantra of the Inconceivable Secret. Cakrasaṃvara-
  guhyācintyatantra. 'Khor lo sdom pa gsang ba bsam gyis mi khyab pa'i
  rgyud kyi rgyal po.* Toh 385, rgyud *ga.* 196a1–199a1.

Compendium of Truths. Tattvasaṃgraha. De kho na nyid bsdus pa. Toh
  479, rgyud *nya.* 1b1–142a7.

*Eight-Thousand-Verse Perfection of Wisdom Sutra. Aṣṭasāhasrikāpra-
  jñāpāramitā. Shes rab pha rol tu phyin pa brgyad stong pa.* Toh 12,
  sher phyin *ka.* 1b1–286a6.

*Enlightenment of Vairocana. Mahāvairocanābhisambodhi. Rnam par
  snang mdzad chen po mngon par rdzogs par byang chub pa.* Toh 494,
  rgyud *tha.* 151b2–260a7.

Hevajratantra. Kye'i rdo rje zhes bya ba rgyud kyi rgyal po. Toh 417,
  rgyud *nga.* 1b1–13b5.

*Kāśyapa Chapter. Kāśyapaparivartasūtra. 'Od srungs gis zhus pa lung
  bstan pa mdo.* Toh 87, dkon brtsegs *cha.* 119b1–151b7. Chapter 43 of
  the *Ratnakuṭa Sutra* collection.

*King of Samādhis Sutra. Samādhirājasūtra. Ting nge 'dzin rgyal po'i
  mdo.* Toh 127, mdo sde *da.* 1b1–170b7.

*Secret Essence Tantra. Guhyagarbhatantra. Gsang ba'i snying po de kho
  na nyid rnam par nges pa.* Toh 832, rnying rgyud *kha.* 110b1–132a7.

*Secret Lamp of Wisdom Tantra. Jñānaguhyadīparatnopadeśatantra. Ye
  shes gsang ba sgron ma man ngag rin po che'i rgyud.* In *Rnying ma'i rgyud
  'bum,* vol. 4, 2–24. Thimbu, Bhutan: Dingo Khyentse Rimpoche, 1975.

Sutra of the Excellent Night. Bhadrakarātrisūtra. Mtshan mo bzang po.
  Toh 313, mdo sde *sa.* 161b1–163b5.

Ten Wheels of Kṣitigarbha Sutra. Daśacakrakṣitigarbhasūtra. Chen

po las sa'i snying po'i 'khor lo bcu pa. Toh 239, mdo sde *zha.*
100a1–241b4.

Wisdom upon Passing Away Sutra. Atyayajñānasūtra. 'Da' ka ye shes.
Toh 122, mdo sde *tha.* 153a1–153b1.

Tengyur (Canonical Treatises)

Aśvaghoṣa. *A Letter of Consolation. Śokavinodana. Mya ngan bsal ba.*
Toh 4177, spring yig' *nge.* 34a3–35b2.

Forty Mahāsiddhas. *Creation of Vajra Songs: A Golden Garland of the
Adorning Marks of Instructions. *Vajragītibhāvanopadeśatilaka-
kanakamālā. Rdo rje'i mgur bzhengs pa nyams kyi man ngag thig le
gser gyi phreng ba.* Toh 2449, rgyud *zi.* 83a1–85b6.

Kamalaśīla. *Letterless Mahāmudrā. Mahāmudrātattvānākṣaropadeśa.
De kho na nyid phyag rgya chen po yi ge med pa'i man ngag.* Toh 2325,
rgyud *zhi.* 266b2–267b2.

Maitreyanātha. *Distinguishing the Middle Way from the Extremes.
Madhyāntavibhāga. Dbus dang mtha' rnam par 'byed pa.* Toh 4021,
sems tsam *phi.* 40b1–45a6.

———. *Sublime Continuum. Mahāyāna Uttaratantraśāstra. Theg
pa chen po rgyud bla ma'i bstan bcos.* Toh 4024, sems tsam *phi.*
54b1–73a7. Also known as *Ratnagotravibhāga.*

———. *Ornament of the Mahayana Sutras. Mahāyanasūtrālaṃkāra.
Mdo sde rgyan.* Toh 4020, sems tsam *phi.* 1a1–39a4.

Nāgārjuna. *Letter to a Friend. Suhṛllekha. Bshes pa'i sprin yig.* Toh 4182,
spring yig *nge.* 40b4–46b3.

———. *Praise to the Dharmadhātu. Dharmadhātustava. Chos kyi dbyings su bstod pa.* Toh 1118, bstod tshogs *ka.* 63b5–67b3.

Nāropa. *Summary of the View. Dṛṣṭisaṃkṣipta. Lta ba mdor bsdus pa.*
Toh 2304, rgyud *zhi.* 244a5–245b3.

Śāntideva. *Entering the Conduct of a Bodhisattva. Bodhicaryāvatāra. Byang
chub sems dpa'i spyod pa la 'jug pa.* Toh 3871, dbu ma *la.* 1a1–40a7.

Saraha. *Treasury of Dohas. Dohakoṣagīti. Do ha mdzod kyi glu.* Toh
2224, rgyud *wi.* 70b5–77a3.

Tailikapāda (Tilopa). *Mahāmudrā Instructions. Mahāmudropadeśa.
Phyag rgya chen po'i man ngag.* Toh 2303, rgyud *zhi.* 242b7–244a5.

Vasubandhu. *Treatise on the Five Aggregates. Pañcaskandhaprakaraṇa,* Toh 4059 Tengyur, sems tsam, *shi.* 11b4–17a7.

TIBETAN WORKS

Dampa Sangye. (Dam pa sangs rgyas) *The Essence of a Precious Portion of the Tantras: A Secret "Paciifying Suffering" Text. Dam chos sdug bsngal zhi byed kyi gzhung gsang ba bsam gyi mi khyab pa'i rgyud sde'i dum bu rin po che'i snying po.* In Jamgön Kongtrul, *The Treasury of Instructions (Gdams ngag mdzod),* vol. 13 (*pa*), 1a–19b1. Delhi: Shechen Publications, 1999.

Gampopa Sönam Rinchen (Sgam po pa Bsod rnams rin chen). *Treasury of the Ultimate: Introduction to the Essence. Snying po'i ngo sprod don dam gter mdzod.* In *Collected Works of Sgam po pa Bsod rnams rin chen,* vol. *ga,* section *ra.* Kathmandu: Khenpo S. Tenzin and Lama T. Namgyal, 2000.

———. *Ornament of Precious Liberation: Like a Wish-Fulfilling Gem of Sublime Dharma. Dam chos yid bzhin nor bu thar pa rin po che'i rgyan.* In *Rtsib ri spar ma,* vol. 1: 33–479. Darjeeling: Kagyu Sungrab Nyamso Khang, 1975–85.

Gyalwa Yangönpa (Rgyal ba yang dgon pa). *The Great Tantra that Teaches Unimpeded Dzogchen. Rdzogs pa chen po zang thal du bstan pa'i rgyud chen mo.* In *Teachings on the Unimpeded Realization of Dzogchen (Rdzogs pa chen po dgongs pa zang thal gyi chos skor),* vol. 3. Delhi: Tashigang, 1979.

Kunga Rinchen (Kun dga' rin chen). *Opening the Eyes of the Innate Mahāmudrā View.* In *The Collected Teachings of Lord Kunga Rinchen (Rje kun dga' rin chen gyi 8 bka' 'bum),* vols. 53–56 of *The Great Dharma Treasury of the Drigung Kagyü ('Bri gung bka' brgyud chos mdzod chen mo),* vol. 54 (yi), 38b–61a. Lhasa: n.p., 2004.

Lingchen Repa Pema Dorjé (Gling chen ras pa Pad ma rdo rje). *Collected Works of Lingchen Repa Pema Dorjé. Gling chen ras pa padma rdo rje'i gsung 'bum.* India: Khams pa sgar gsung rab nyams gdo khang, 1985.

Mikyö Dorjé (Mi bskyod rdo rje). *The Transmission of Glorious Düsum Khyenpa: A Commentary on [Candrakīrti's] "Entering the Middle Way."* Palpung Monastery, n.d.

Ngari Tertön Garwang Dorjé (Mnga' ris gter ston Gar dbang rdo rje). *Mahāmudrā: Seeing the Naked Intrinsic Nature. Phyag chen gnyug ma gcer mthong.* Delhi: Lama Dawa, 1983.

Sangyé Lingpa (Sangs rgyas gling pa). *Unity of the Gurus' Realization. Bla ma dgongs 'dus.* 13 vols. Gangtok: Sonam Topgay Kazi, 1972.

Tenzin Dönkun Drupai Dé (Bstan 'dzin don kun grub pa'i sde). *The Excellent Path that Leads to the Great Akaniṣṭha: Instructions on the Main Practice of the Mahāmudrā Innate Union. Phyag rgya chen po lhan cig skyes sbyor dngos gzhi'i khrid yig 'og min chen por bgrod pa'i lam bzang,* In *The Great Dharma Treasury of the Drukpa Tradition* ('*Drug lugs chos mdzod chen po*), vol. 46 (*pa*) 593a–726b. Kathmandu: Drukpa Kagyu Heritage Project, n.d.

Wangchuk Gyaltsen (Dbang phyug rgyal mtshan). *Great Bliss of Stainless Teachings: A Biography of Nāropa. Nā ro pa'i rnam thar dri med legs bshad bde chen.* Palampur, H.P., India: Sungrab nyamso gyunphel parkhang, 1972–76.

Yeshé Jungné (Ye shes 'byung gnas). *The Methods for Entering the Mahāyāna Yoga. Theg pa chen po'i rnal 'byor la 'jug pa'i thabs bye brag tu 'byed pa.* In *The Extensive Instructions* (*Bka' ma shin tu rgyas pa*), vol. 59 (*hi*), 1a–22a. Chengdu: Kaḥ thog mkhan po 'jam dbyangs, 1999.

Works Cited by the Translator

Aris, Michael. *Bhutan: The Early History of a Himalayan Kingdom.* Warminster, England: Aris and Phillips, 1979.

Brown, Daniel P. *Pointing Out the Great Way: The Stages of Meditation in the Mahāmudrā Tradition.* Boston: Wisdom Publications, 2006.

Chang, Garma C. C. *The Six Yogas of Naropa and Teachings on Mahamudra.* Ithaca, NY: Snow Lion Publications, 1986.

Cozort, Daniel. *Highest Yoga Tantra.* Ithaca, NY: Snow Lion Publications, 1986.

Dakpo Tashi Namgyal. *Clarifying the Natural State: A Principal Guidance Manual for Mahamudra.* Trans. Erik Pema Kunsang. Hong Kong: Rangjung Yeshe Publications, 2001.

———. *Mahāmudrā: The Moonlight—Quintessence of Mind and Meditation.* Trans. Lobsang Lhalungpa. Boston: Wisdom Publications, 2006.

Davidson, Ronald M. *Indian Esoteric Buddhism.* New York: Columbia University Press, 2003.

Dorjé Dzeö (Rdo rje mdzes 'od). *The Precious Treasury that Is the Source of All that Is Required: Great Kagyü Biographies. Bka' brgyud kyi rnam thar chen mo rin po che'i gter mdzod dgos 'dod 'byung gnas.* Kangra, H.P., India: Tzondu Senghe, 1985.

Dorje, Sherab. *The Eighth Situpa on the Third Karmapa's Mahamudra Prayer.* Ithaca: Snow Lion Publications, 2004.

Ducher, Cécile. *Building Tradition: The Lives of Mar-pa the Translator.* Munich: Indus Verlag, 2014.

Evans-Wentz, W. Y., ed. *Tibetan Yoga and Secret Doctrines.* London: Oxford University Press, 1935.

Gö Lotsāwa Shönu Pal ('Gos lo tsā ba Gzhon nu dpal). *The Blue Annals.* Trans. George N. Roerich. Calcutta: Motilal Banarsidass, 1949.

Gyalthangpa Dechen Dorjé (Gyal thang pa [Rgya ldang pa] Bde chen rdo rje). *Golden Succession of the Kagyü. Dkar brgyud gser phreng.* Tashijong, Palampur, H.P., India: Sungrab Nyamso Gyunphel Parkhang, 1973.

Jamgön Kongtrul Lodrö Thayé. *Creation and Completion: Essential Points of Tantric Meditation.* Trans. Sarah Harding. Boston: Wisdom Publications, 1996.

———. ('Jam mgon kong sprul Blo gros mtha' yas). *The Treasury of Knowledge. Shes bya kun khyab (Theg pa'i sgo kun las btus pa gsung rab rin po che'i mdzod bslab pa gsum legs par ston pa'i bstan bcos shes bya kun khyab),* 3 vols. Xining: Mi rigs Dpe skrun khang, 1982.

———. *The Treasury of Knowledge, book 6, part 3: Frameworks of Buddhist Philosophy: A Systematic Presentation of the Cause-Based Philosophical Vehicles.* Trans. Elizabeth M. Callahan. Ithaca, NY: Snow Lion Publications, 2007.

———. *The Treasury of Knowledge, book 8, part 3: The Elements of Tantric Practice: A General Exposition of the Process of Meditation in the Indestructible Way of Secret Mantra.* Trans. Elio Guarisco and Ingrid McLeod. Ithaca, NY: Snow Lion Publications, 2008.

———. *The Treasury of Knowledge, book 8, part 4: Esoteric Instructions:*

A Detailed Presentation of the Process of Meditation in Vajrayāna.
Trans. Sarah Harding. Ithaca, NY: Snow Lion Publications, 2007.

Karmapa Wangchuk Dorjé. *Mahāmudrā: The Ocean of Definitive Meaning.* Trans. Elizabeth Callahan. Seattle: Nitartha, 2001.

———. *The Mahāmudrā: Eliminating the Darkness of Ignorance.* Trans. Alexander Berzin. Dharamsala: Library of Tibetan Works and Archives, 1978.

Kathok Tsewang Norbu (Kaḥ thog tshe dbang nor bu). *Clear Brief Correct Account of Definite Chronology: Seeds of the Biographies of Some Holy Beings, such as Marpa, Milarepa, and Gampopa. Mar mi dwags po jo bo rje yab sras sogs dam pa 'ga' zhig gi rnam thar sa bon dus kyi nges pa brjod pa dag ldan nyung gsal.* In *Kathok Rikzin Tsewang Norbu's Collected Works. Kaḥ thog rig 'dzin tshe dbang nor bu'i bka' 'bum,* vol. 3, 640–54. Beijing: Krung go'i bod rig pa dpe skrun khang, 2006.

Larsson, Stefan. *Crazy for Wisdom: The Making of a Mad Yogi in Fifteenth-Century Tibet.* Leiden: Brill, 2012.

[Lhatsun Rinchen Namgyal]. *The Life and Teaching of Naropa.* Trans. Herbert V. Guenther. Boston: Shambhala Publications, 1986.

Lusthaus, Dan. *Buddhist Phenomenology: A Philosophical Investigation of Yogācāra.* London: Routledge Curzon, 2002.

Martin, Dan. "A Twelfth-Century Tibetan Classic of Mahāmudrā: The Path of Ultimate Profundity: The Great Seal Instructions of Zhang." *The Journal of the International Association of Buddhist Studies* 15.2 (1992): 243–319.

Mullin, Glenn H. *The Practice of the Six Yogas of Naropa.* Ithaca, NY: Snow Lion Publications, 1997.

Quintman, Andrew. *The Yogin and the Madman: Reading the Biographical Corpus of Tibet's Great Saint Milarepa.* New York: Columbia University Press, 2014.

Rangjung Dorjé, Karmapa (Rang byung rdo rje). *Treatise Differentiating Consciousnesses and Wisdom. Rnam shes dang ye shes 'byed pa'i bstan bcos.* In *Karma pa rang byung rdo rje'i gsung 'bum,* vol. 7, 275–82. Zi ling: Tshur phu mkhan po lo yag bkra shis, 2006.

Roberts, Peter Alan. *The Biographies of Rechungpa: The Evolution of a Tibetan Hagiography.* Abingdon, Oxon: Routledge, 2007.

———. "The Evolution of the Biographies of Milarepa and Rechungpa."

In *Lives Lived, Lives Imagined: Biography in the Buddhist Traditions*, ed. Linda Covill et al., 181–203. Boston: Wisdom Publications, 2010.

———. *Mahāmudrā and Related Instructions: Core Teachings of the Kagyü School*. Boston: Wisdom Publications, 2011.

Schaeffer, Kurtis R. *Dreaming the Great Brahmin: Tibetan Traditions of the Buddhist Poet-Saint Saraha*. Oxford: Oxford University Press, 2004.

Stewart, Jampa Mackenzie. *The Life of Gampopa*. Ithaca, NY: Snow Lion Publications, 1995.

Tatsak Tsewang Gyal (Rta tshag Tshe dbang rgyal). *The Dharma History from Lhorong (The Marvelous, Rare, Special Text Known by the Name of the Place Where It Was Written: An Excellent Description of the History of the Dharma, Known as "The Dharma History from Lhorong" or "The Dharma History from Tatsak")*. *Lho rong chos 'byung (Dam pa'i chos kyi byung ba'i legs bshad lho rong chos 'byung gnam rta tshag chos 'byung zhes rtsom pa'i yul ming du chags pa'i ngo mtshar zhing dkon pa'i dpe khyed par can)*. Mtsho sngon (Quinghai): Bod ljongs bod yig dpe rnying dpe skrun khang, 1994.

Thinley, Karma. *The History of the Sixteen Karmapas of Tibet*. Boulder, CO: Prajna Press, 1980.

Tola, Fernando, and Carmen Dragonetti. *Being as Consciousness: Yogācāra Philosophy of Buddhism*. Delhi: Motilal Banarsidass, 2006.

Tsangnyön Heruka. *The Hundred Thousand Songs of Milarepa*. Trans. Garma C. C. Chang. Boston: Shambhala Publications, 1989.

———. *The Life of Marpa the Translator: Seeing All Accomplishes All*. Trans. Nalanda Translation Committee. Boston: Shambhala Publications, 1982.

———. *The Life of Milarepa*. Trans. Andrew Quintman. New York: Penguin, 2010.

Tselé Natsok Rangdröl (Rtse le sna tshogs rang grol, b. 1608). *Answers to Mengom's Questions. Sman sgom gyi dris lan gnyis chos zung 'jug gi ngo sprod zhal gdams*. In Collected Works, vol. 4, 515–36. Gangtok: Mgon po tshe brtan, 1979.

———. *Lamp of Mahamudra*. Trans. Erik Pema Kunsang. Boston: Shambhala Publications, 1989.

Yeshe, Lama Thubten. *The Bliss of Inner Fire: Heart Practice of the Six Yogas of Naropa*. Boston: Wisdom Publications, 1998.

Index

About the Contributors

PETER ALAN ROBERTS was born in Wales and lives in Hollywood, California. He obtained a BA in Sanskrit and Pali and a PhD in Tibetan studies from Oxford University (Harris-Manchester College). For more than thirty years he has been an interpreter for lamas and a translator of Tibetan texts. He specializes in the literature of the Kagyü and Nyingma traditions with a focus on tantric practices and is the author of *The Biographies of Rechungpa: The Evolution of a Tibetan Hagiography* (2007).

GESHE THUPTEN JINPA was trained as a monk at the Shartse College of Ganden Monastic University, South India, where he received the Geshe Lharam degree. Jinpa also holds a BA with honors in philosophy and a PhD in religious studies, both from Cambridge University, England. Jinpa has been the principal English-language translator for His Holiness the Dalai Lama for over two decades and has translated and edited numerous books by the Dalai Lama. He is president of the Institute of Tibetan Classics in Montreal, an adjunct professor at McGill University, and chair of the Mind and Life Institute.

About Wisdom Publications

WISDOM PUBLICATIONS is the leading publisher of classic and contemporary Buddhist books and practical works on mindfulness. Publishing books from all major Buddhist traditions, Wisdom is a nonprofit charitable organization dedicated to cultivating Buddhist voices the world over, advancing critical scholarship, and preserving and sharing Buddhist literary culture.

To learn more about us or to explore our other books, please visit our website at www.wisdompubs.org. You can subscribe to our eNewsletter, request a print catalog, and find out how you can help support Wisdom's mission either online or by writing to:

Wisdom Publications
199 Elm Street
Somerville, Massachusetts 02144 USA

You can also contact us at 617-776-7416 or info@wisdompubs.org.

Wisdom is a 501(c)(3) organization, and donations in support of our mission are tax deductible.

Wisdom Publications is affiliated with the Foundation for the Preservation of the Mahayana Tradition (FPMT).

More from the *Tibetan Classics* series

Essential Mind Training
Translated and introduced by Thupten Jinpa
296 pages, $16.95, ebook $12.35

"The clarity and raw power of these
thousand-year-old teachings of the great
Kadampa masters are astonishingly fresh."
—*Buddhadharma*

Wisdom of the Kadam Masters
Translated and introduced by Thupten Jinpa
232 pages, $16.95, ebook $12.35

"Thupten Jinpa shines as an interpreter of classical Buddhism for
our times. In *Wisdom of the Kadam Masters* he shows
how these pithy sayings from long ago offer anyone sound
principles for living a meaningful, fulfilling, and happy life."
—Daniel Goleman, author of *Emotional Intelligence*

Also Available from Wisdom Publications

Mahāmudrā and Related Instructions
Core Teachings of the Kagyü Schools
Translated by Peter Alan Roberts
800 pages, $59.95, ebook $34.99

"This collection is a treasury from the most renowned gurus of the Mahāmudrā lineage. Every page exudes freshness of realization, holding the keys to our own personal awakening."
—Judith Simmer-Brown, author of *Dakini's Warm Breath*

Essentials of Mahāmudrā
Looking Directly at the Mind
Khenchen Thrangu Rinpoche
288 pages, $18.95, ebook $13.81

"Makes the practice of mahāmudrā easily acessible to Westerners' everyday lives. A wonderful way of bringing us to the path."
—*Mandala*

Mahāmudrā
The Moonlight—Quintessence of Mind and Meditation
Dakpo Tashi Namgyal
Translated and annotated by Lobsang P. Lhalungpa
Foreword by His Holiness the Dalai Lama
528 pages, $34.95

"A fundamentally valuable addition to one's Dharma library."
—*Mandala*